New Edition

Viewfinder

Topics

The Global Village

Progress or Disaster?

compiled and edited
by
Laurenz Volkmann

L

Langenscheidt

Berlin · Madrid · München · Warschau · Wien · Zürich

Viewfinder
Topics – New Edition plus

Unterrichtsmaterialien für die Sekundarstufe II

The Global Village

Progress or Disaster?

Herausgeber:
Prof. em. Dr. Dr. h.c. Dr. h.c. Peter Freese

Autor:
Prof. Dr. Laurenz Volkmann

Projekt-Team:
Dr. Martin Arndt, Münster
Prof. Dr. Mita Banerjee, Mainz
David Beal, M. A., Bochum
Cornelia Becker, Bremen
Dr. Peter Dines, Cert. Ed., Ludwigsburg
Prof. Dr. Hanspeter Dörfel †
Prof. Dr. Sabine Doff, Bremen
Dr. Claudia Drawe, Essen
OStR Dieter Düwel, Castrop-Rauxel
Prof. em. Dr. Dr. h.c. mult. Peter Freese, Paderborn
Dr. Christine Gottstein-Strobl, Eichstätt
Dr. Nancy Grimm, Jena
Jennifer von der Grün, B. A., Dortmund
OStR Ulrich Imig, Wildeshausen
OStR Reimer Jansen, Oyten-Sagehorn
Dr. Michael Mitchell, M. A., Reken und Warwick
Prof. Dr. Michael Porsche, Paderborn
Dr. Peter-J. Rekowski, Kirchhain
StD i. K. Peter Ringeisen, M. A., Amberg
StD Karl Sassenberg, Münster
StD Dr. Annegret Schrick, Essen
OStR Ekkehard Sprenger, Kiel
StR Susanne Stadler, Wiesbaden
OStD Dr. Dietrich Theißen †
Prof. Dr. Laurenz Volkmann, Jena

Verlagsredaktion: Dr. Beatrix Finke
Visuelles Konzept: Barbara Slowik, Atelier S., München
Layout und Produktion: kaltner verlagsmedien GmbH, Bobingen

www.langenscheidt.de/viewfinder

Druck und Bindung: Stürtz GmbH Würzburg
ISBN 978-3-526-51048-2

13010

Contents

The Global

• Playing bridge with Siberia

In the summer of 1998 my then seventy-nine-year-old mother, Margaret Friedman, who lives in Minneapolis, called me sounding very upset. "What's wrong, Mom?" I asked. "Well," she said, "I've been playing bridge on the internet with three Frenchmen and they keep speaking French to each other and I can't understand them." When I chuckled at the thought of my card-shark mom playing bridge with three Frenchmen on the Net, she took a little umbrage. "Don't laugh," she said, "I was playing bridge with someone in Siberia the other day."

(Thomas L. Friedman in his book The Lexus and the Olive Tree, *p. xix, cf. p. 19)*

• Globalization wears Mickey Mouse ears

Today, globalization often wears Mickey Mouse ears, eats Big Macs, drinks Coke or Pepsi and does its computing on an IBM PC, using Windows 98, with an Intel Pentium II processor and a network link from Cisco Systems. Therefore, while the distinction between what is globalization and what is Americanization may be clear to most Americans, it is not – unfortunately – to many others around the world.

(Friedman, The Lexus and the Olive Tree, *p. 382)*

• Hopes of the Pepsi-Generation of Russia

Once upon a time in Russia, there really was a carefree, youthful generation that smiled in joy at the summer, the sea and the sun, and chose Pepsi. (...) No matter which way it was, as the children lounged on the seashore in the summer, gazing endlessly at a cloudless blue horizon, they drank warm Pepsi-Cola decanted into glass bottles in the city of Novorossiisk and dreamed that some day the distant forbidden world on the far side of the sea would be part of their own lives.

(Victor Pelevin in his novel Babylon, *translated from the Russian in 1999, p. 3)*

Vocabulary

upset (adj.): unhappy and angry – **chuckle** (v.): /'tʃʌkl/ laugh quietly – **card-shark** (n.): (humorous usage) someone who uses their skill at cards to cheat other players out of money – **take umbrage**: /'ʌmbrɪdʒ/ be offended by something that someone has done or said, often without good reason – **distinction** (n.): a clear difference or separation between two similar things – **lounge** (v.): stand, sit, or lie in a lazy or relaxed way – **gaze** (v.): look at someone or something for a long time, giving it all your attention, often without realizing you are doing so – **Novorossiisk**: a harbour by the Black Sea, an industrial city of the Ukraine

Village

• The forces of history?

Globalization is inevitable and irreversible.
(Tony Blair, British Prime Minister, in a speech, 2003, qtd. in New York Times *[international ed.], May 2, 2005, p. 2)*

• Global economy

If you're totally illiterate and living on one dollar a day, the benefits of globalization never come to you.
(Jimmy Carter, former President of the USA, http://www.finestquotes.com*)*

Instead of having a set of policies that are equipping people for the globalization of the economy, we have policies that are accelerating the most destructive trends of the global economy. *(Barack Obama, President of the USA,* ThinkExist.com*)*

• Global terror

For most Americans, the age of globalization or interdependence has brought enormous benefits. (...) Though it worked for us, interdependence is not by definition good or bad. It can be either or; it can be both. On September 11th, 2001, the Al Quaeda terrorists used the forces of interdependence – they used the open borders, easy travel, easy immigration, easy access to information and technology, to turn a jet airplane full of fuel into a weapon of mass destruction to kill 3100 people in the United States, including hundreds of people from 70 foreign countries who were in America looking for positive interdependence. Over 200 of the people they killed were Muslims, indicating the racial and religious diversity of the positive side of this equation.
(Bill Clinton, former President of the USA, in a speech, 2003)

inevitable (adj.): /ɪnˈevɪtəbl/ certain to happen and impossible to avoid – **irreversible** (adj.): /ˌɪrɪˈvɜːsəbl/ a change is so serious or so great that you cannot change something back to how it was before – **interdependence** (n.): a situation in which people or things depend on each other – **Al Quaeda**: an international terrorist network, held responsible for the 9 / 11 attacks – **access** (v.): find information, especially on a computer – **diversity** (n.): a range of different people, things, or ideas – **equation** (n.): /ɪˈkweɪʒən/ the set of different facts, ideas, or people that all affect a situation and must be considered together

Globalization: Some Definitions

DEFINITION 1

The process of making something such as a business operate in a lot of different countries all around the world, or the result of this.

(DCE)

DEFINITION 2

We can therefore define globalization as: A social process in which the constraints of geography on social and cultural arrangements recede and in which people become increasingly aware that they are receding.

(Malcolm Waters, Globalization. London, 1995, p. 3)

DEFINITION 3

Only a few years ago the term "globalization" was hardly used. Now one comes across it everywhere. The global spread of the term is evidence of the very changes it describes. Something very new is happening in the world. Four basic trends are involved. The first is the world-wide communications revolution. After the first satellite was sent up above the earth in the late 1960s, which made instantaneous world-wide communication possible, there has been an enormous intensification of global communications, with the internet as the latest and most profound change. The second dramatic change is the arrival of the "weightless economy", a new "knowledge economy" which operates according to global, not national principles. This is most striking in the financial sector and how financial markets operate. Thirdly, globalization refers to a post-1989 world. The fall of Soviet Communism initiated one of the most drastic transformations of the century. The Soviet Union simply could not compete in the new global electronic economy. Finally, globalization has its effects on the level of everyday life. One of the biggest changes of the past thirty years is the growing equality between men and women, a trend that is worldwide, even if it still has a long way to go. This development is connected with changes affecting the family and emotional life more generally, not only in Western societies but almost everywhere.

(Interview with Anthony Giddens, director of the London School of Economics, 2000)

Vocabulary

DCE: Dictionary of Contemporary English – **constraint** (n.): barrier – **arrangement** (n.): the way in which something is organized – **recede** (v.): /rɪˈsiːd/ grow smaller – **evidence** (n.): words which prove a statement, support or belief, or make a matter more clear – **intensification** (n.): becoming stronger – **profound** (adj.): deep, strong – **transformation** (n.): changing completely in form, appearance, or nature – **affect** (v.) /əˈfekt/ influence, cause some result or influence in

ANALYSIS

1 Analyse how each definition works and differs from the others.

INTERNET PROJECT

2 Go to the following websites to get more information on globalization. In most cases, you can download papers on the issue. Compare the different political angles.

GENERAL WEBSITES:
www.migrationinformation.com
www.globalpolicy.org
www.equalitytoday.org

PAPERS:
www.imf.org/external/np/exr/ib/2000/041200.htm#II
ilectric.com/glance/Society/Politics/Globalization/Theory
www.iatp.irex.am/grants/globalization
www.nd.edu/~kellogg/WPS/261.pdf
www.globalisationguide.org/sb02.html

The Shrinking Map of the World

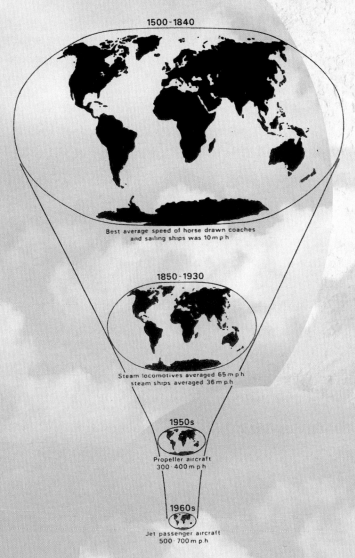

1500-1840

Best average speed of horse drawn coaches and sailing ships was 10 m p h

1850-1930

Steam locomotives averaged 65 m p h steam ships averaged 36 m p h

1950s

Propeller aircraft 300 400 m p h

1960s

Jet passenger aircraft 500 700 m p h

The shrinking map of the world through innovations in transport which 'annihilate space through time' (Source: David Harvey, The Condition of Postmodernity. *Cambridge MA: Blackwell, 1996, 245).*

Vocabulary

shrink (v.): become smaller – **annihilate** (v.): /əˈnaɪəleɪt/ cause to disappear

AWARENESS

1 The term "global village" was introduced by the Canadian media specialist and philosopher Marshall McLuhan. What exactly does the term signify? Has this world become a village to you?

COMPREHENSION

2 Look at the excerpts and quotes on the preceding pages. Then describe how they contribute to an understanding of globalization.
3 Describe the idea behind the diagram "the shrinking map of the world". What does it illustrate?

ANALYSIS

4 Take a second look at the excerpts and quotes on the preceding pages. Then assess how they express feelings of hope or fear.
5 The diagram "The shrinking map of the world" ends in the 1960s. Find a way to describe how recent innovations have furthered the "shrinking of the world".

OPINION

6 Which quote characterizes the process of globalization best? Why?
7 Give some examples how the world has shrunk for you. What are the advantages, what are the disadvantages (for you)?

PROJECT

8 Write a short paragraph or statement giving an instance from your life which could characterize the global village. Use all the statements from your class/group and make a collage of them. Discuss what they have in common.

1

Historical Survey – Timeline

Many historians and sociologists have asked the question when globalization began or where it had its historical roots. The chart below provides a survey of the main historical trends leading to globalization. Six phases are described here. – The survey is based on Malcolm Waters, *Globalization* (London / New York: Routledge, 1995), 43–45.

I The early-development phase (Europe, 1400–1750)

- Christendom dissolves, state communities emerge
- Catholic (that is, universal) churches
- development of generalizations about humanity and the individual
- first maps of the planet
- sun-centred universe
- universal calendar in the West
- global exploration
- colonialism

II The beginning phase (Europe, 1750–1875)

- nation-state
- formal diplomacy between states
- citizenship and passports
- international exhibitions and communications agreements
- international legal conventions
- first non-European nations
- first ideas of internationalism and universalism

III The take-off phase (1875–1925)

- concept of the world in terms of the four globalizing reference points – the nation-state, the individual, a single international society, and a single (masculine) humanity
- international communications, sporting and cultural links
- global calendar
- first ever world war
- mass international migrations and restrictions thereon
- more non-Europeans in the international club of nation-states

| TIME | 1400 | 1750 | 1875 |

Vocabulary

legal convention: a pact, law or formal agreement, especially between countries, about particular rules or behaviour – **universalism** (n.): the idea that certain rules and beliefs involve everyone in the world – **hegemony** (n.): /hɪˈgemənɪ/ a situation in which one state or country controls others – **emerge** (v.): /ɪˈmɜːdʒ/ to appear or come out – **nuclear threat**: the threat posed by nuclear bombs and destruction, possibly of the whole globe – **sexual preference**: decisions taken on the basis of one's sexuality, whether one is heterosexual or homosexual – **ethnicity** (n.): belonging to a particular race, nation, or tribe and being rooted in their customs and traditions

IV The struggle-for-hegemony phase (1925–69)

- League of Nations and UN
- Second World War; Cold War
- conceptions of war crimes and crimes against humanity
- the universal nuclear threat of the atomic bomb
- emergence of the Third (part of the) World

V The uncertainty phase (1969–92)

- exploration of space
- post-materialist values and rights discourses
- world communities based on sexual preference, gender, ethnicity and race
- international relations more complex and flexible
- global environmental problems recognized
- global mass media via space technology (satellite television etc.)

VI Globalization (now)

- the uncertainty phase continues
- spread of multinational corporations
- spread of capitalism, end of communism
- mobility and exchange of information increases even further
- beginning of the Information Technology Age (internet, e-mail, mobile phones), allowing simultaneous exchange of information worldwide
- post-national structures develop
- the Digital Revolution

| 1925 | 1969 | 1992 | 2000 |

AWARENESS

1   Look at the pictures and timeline above. Try to visualize history as a process leading up to your life. Then try to fit the pictures into a historical context.

COMPREHENSION

2   Where do you see the main differences between the six phases?
3   How does each phase lead to the next?
4   Make sure you understand all the terms used here. You may want to consult a dictionary or a history book (or the internet, for that matter). What, for example, is meant by 'post-materialist' values?

5 Charts like these give the impression of history as a constant, logical development. Is this true in reality? Did history have to develop this way?

6 Look at each aspect of the six phases and try to give exact dates and events, using an encyclopedia or history book (see above). For example, with the term "global exploration" (phase 1) you could write down: "1492: Christophorus Columbus 'discovers' America".

OPINION

7 Think about what life was like and how it was different from today in each phase. Would you have liked to live in a phase before globalization?

8 Is globalization an 'improvement' compared to earlier phases?

PROJECT

9 Find out more about the years after 1989 (the collapse of Communism). Draw your own timeline, including all major trends and events which have given a push to globalization recently.

A Satirical Look at the World

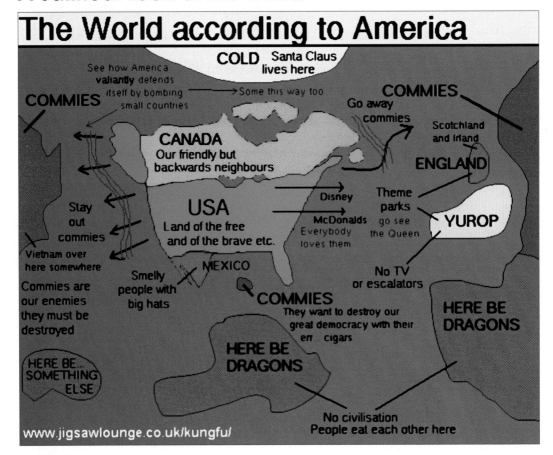

Vocabulary

Here be dragons: Alluding to a traditional phrase used by early mapmakers that a region was unexplored and potentially dangerous – **valiant** (adj.): /'væliənt/ very brave, esp. in war

ANALYSIS

1 Explain the cartoon in detail. Keep in mind that its correct headline should be "The world according to the USA". Explain its humour – it helps to consider US-American history.

PROJECT

2 What would your map of the world look like? Draw one and compare it with those of others.

B. B. Kachru, David Crystal

2

The Family Tree of English – Three Circles of English

English is increasingly becoming the *lingua franca* – the language of international communication – in the global village. Historically, English has attained its privileged status primarily as the result of two factors: the expansion of British colonial power, which peaked towards the end of the nineteenth century, and the emergence of the United States as the leading economic power of the 20th century. It is the latter factor which continues to explain the world position of the English language today.

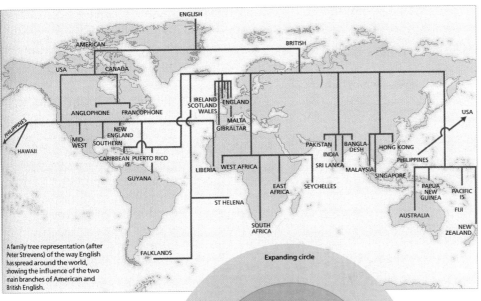

Family Tree of English

A family tree representation of the way English has spread around the world, showing the influence of the two main branches of American and British English.

A family tree representation (after Peter Strevens) of the way English has spread around the world, showing the influence of the two main branches of American and British English.

Three Circles

The spread of English can be visualized as three concentric circles, representing different ways in which the language has been acquired and is currently used. (1) The inner circle refers to the traditional bases of English – English is the primary language. (2) In the outer or extended circle

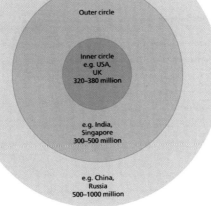

Expanding circle

Outer circle

Inner circle
e.g. USA,
UK
320–380 million

e.g. India,
Singapore
300–500 million

e.g. China,
Russia
500–1000 million

English has become part of the country's chief institutions; it fulfils an important "second language role" in multilingual settings. (3) In the expanding circle or extending circle the importance of English is recognized as an international language.

Awareness

1 How many varieties of English do you know? Can you describe how they differ from each other?

Comprehension

2 Describe the spread of English, using your own words.

Analysis

3 Discuss the problems of Kachru's model with regard to different language skills.

Opinion

4 Are native speakers automatically the best speakers of English?
5 Which English has the most prestige and authority? Is this changing? Are there Englishes which have little prestige? Why?

3

David Crystal

Why English?

Today, Great Britain and the USA have about 70 percent of all native speakers of English. On a worldwide scale, English is now spoken by more people than any other language and is recognised by more countries as a desirable *lingua franca* than any other language. It is now the predominant language in over 60 countries and is represented in every continent. The spread of English continues, with more than one in five persons in the world having some kind of knowledge of English. According to estimations, by the year 2050, 50 percent of the world population will have some competence in English. In his handbook *The Cambridge Encyclopedia of the English Language* David Crystal, one of the most eminent experts in the field, presents the main reasons for the success story of the English language (2nd ed. Cambridge UP, 2004, 106).

1 If English is not your mother-tongue, why should you want to learn it, or give it special status in your country? There are seven kinds of answer given to this question.

5 **Historical reasons**

Because of the legacy of British or American imperialism, the country's main institutions may carry out their proceedings in English. These include the governing body (e.g. parliament), government agencies, the civil 10 service (at least at senior levels), the law courts, national religious bodies, the schools, and higher educational institutions, along with their related publications (textbooks, proceedings, records, etc.)

15 **Internal political reasons**

Whether a country has imperial antecedents or not, English may have a role in providing a neutral means of communication between its different ethnic groups. A distinctive local variety of English may also become 20 a symbol of national unity or emerging nationhood. The use of English in newspapers, on radio, or on television, adds a further dimension.

External economic reasons

The USA's dominant economic position acts as a magnet 25 for international business and trade, and organizations wishing to develop international markets are thus under considerable pressure to work with English. The tourist and advertising industries are particularly English-dependent, but any multi-national business will wish to 30 establish offices in the major English-speaking countries.

Practical reasons

English is the language of international air traffic control, and is currently developing its role in international 35 maritime, policing, and emergency services […]. It is the chief language of international business and academic conferences, and the leading language of international tourism.

Intellectual reasons

Most of the scientific, technological, and academic 40 information in the world is expressed in English, and over 80 per cent of all the information stored in electronic retrieval systems is in English. Closely related to this is the concern to have access to the philosophical, cultural, religious, and literary history of Western 45 Europe, either directly or through the medium of an English translation. In most parts of the world, the only way most people have access to such authors as Goethe or Dante is through English. […]

Entertainment reasons 50

English is the main language of popular music, and permeates popular culture and its associated advertising. It is also the main language of satellite broadcasting, home computers, and video games, as well as of such international illegal activities as pornography and drugs. 55

Some wrong reasons

It is sometimes thought that English has achieved its worldwide status because of its intrinsic linguistic features. People have claimed that it is inherently a more logical or more beautiful language than others, easier 60 to pronounce, simpler in grammatical structure, or larger in vocabulary. This kind of reasoning is the consequence of chauvinism or naïve linguistic thinking: there are no objective standards of logic or beauty to compare different languages, and questions of phonetic, 65 grammatical, or lexical complexity are never capable of simple answers. For example, English may not have many inflectional endings (which is what most people are thinking of when they talk about English as grammatically 'simple' […]), but it has a highly complex 70 syntax; and the number of endings has no bearing on whether a language becomes used worldwide (as can be seen from the former success of Latin). Languages rise and fall in world esteem for many kinds of reasons – political, economic, social, religious, literary – but 75 linguistic reasons do not rank highly among them.

Vocabulary

6 legacy (n.): /ˈlegəsɪ/ something that happens or exists as a result of things that happened at an earlier time – **8 proceedings** (n.): (plural) record, written minutes – **9 civil service** (n.): the government departments that manage the affairs of the country – **13 record** (n.): information about something that is written down or stored on computer, film etc so that it can be looked at in the future – **16 antecedent** (n.): /ˌæntɪˈsiːdənt/ an event, organization, or thing that is similar to the one you have mentioned but existed earlier – **19 distinctive** (adj.): special – **35 maritime** (adj.): /ˈmærɪtaɪm/ relating to the sea or ships – **35 policing** (n.): the way that an industry or activity etc. is controlled in order to make sure that people obey the rules – **36 chief** (adj.): main – **43 retrieval** (n.) /rɪˈtriːvəl/ (technical) the process of getting back information stored on a computer system – **52 permeate** (v.): /ˈpɜːmieɪt/ if ideas, beliefs, emotions etc permeate something, they are present in every part of it – **52 associated** (adj.): connected with – **58 intrinsic linguistic features**: natural qualities of a language – **59 inherently** (adj.): by nature – **63 chauvinism** (n.): a strong belief that your country or race is better or more important than any other – **68 inflectional** (adj.): referring to the way in which a word changes its form to show a difference in its meaning or use – **71 have no bearing**: have no influence – **74 world esteem** (n.): the quality attributed to it worldwide – **76 rank highly**: be considered of great importance

AWARENESS

1 Think of all the contexts in your everyday life where you need to know at least some English. Write them down.
2 Consider the English words in your everyday language. Make a list of them.

COMPREHENSION

3 Sum up the reasons for the spread of English in your own words.
4 Give one or two examples for each reason, drawing on your experiences abroad or on how English is used in your country.

ANALYSIS

5 Why has the author chosen this order of presenting his reasons?
6 How does the author weigh the various reasons for the spread of English as a global language?

OPINION

7 Do you agree with the author's list of reasons? Which is the most convincing reason for you? Discuss with others.
8 Could you add further reasons for the spread of English? Think of recent technological developments.

PROJECTS

9 Do you think that the language one speaks defines one's (national) identity? Discuss with friends, especially foreign friends, for instance via e-mail.
10 How has English influenced your mother tongue? Is there any resistance to the spread of English in your country?
11 A criticism levelled against the spread of English is that of "language imperialism". Find out about English language teaching as one of the most lucrative international growth businesses and who profits from it.
12 Find out about which language(s) is/are used at official occasions at European Community or UN meetings. Wouldn't it be a lot easier and more efficient to use just English at these meetings?
13 Find out about reasons why nations insist on having their language used at official meetings.

Background Reading

For critical perspectives on the issue of the spread of English, read parts of the following books: Alastair Pennycook, *The Cultural Politics of English as an International Language* (London: Longman, 1994), Robert Phillipson, *Linguistic Imperialism* (Oxford: OUP, 1992). For starters, enter the key phrase "language imperialism" in Google and read some of the definitions.

4

Douglas Adams

The Babel Fish

Douglas Adams (1952–2001) was born in Cambridge, England. The "Babel fish" appears in his hilarious "trilogy" *The Hitchhiker's Guide to the Galaxy*. It was first a British radio programme in 1978, which later became a book and a television programme. It is a science fiction story about an Englishman called Arthur Dent, who gets on a spaceship just before the Earth is destroyed, and the adventures he has in space with the other characters on this spaceship. For intergalactic communication, a fish inserted in the ear is used as an automatic translation device. Its function is explained in the following passage, in which a speaking guide book provides the information. – Douglas Adams, *The Hitchhiker's Guide to the Galaxy: A Trilogy in Four Parts* (London: Heinemann, 1987), 51ff.

1 "What's this fish doing in my ear?"

"It's translating for you. It's a Babel fish. Look it up in the book if you like."

He tossed over *The Hitchhiker's Guide to the Galaxy.*

5 [...]

"The Babel fish," said *The Hitchhiker's Guide to the Galaxy* quietly, "*is small, yellow and leech-like, and probably the oddest thing in the Universe. It feeds on brainwave energy received not from its own carrier but* 10 *from those around it. It absorbs all unconscious mental frequencies from this brainwave energy to nourish itself with. It then excretes into the mind of its carrier a telepathic matrix formed by combining the conscious thought frequencies with nerve signals picked up from the speech centres of the brain which has supplied* 15 *them. The practical upshot of all this is that if you stick a Babel fish in your ear you can instantly understand anything said to you in any form of language. The speech patterns you actually hear decode the brainwave matrix which has been fed into your mind by* 20 *your Babel fish. [...]*

Meanwhile, the poor Babel fish, by effectively removing all barriers to communication between different races and cultures, has caused more and bloodier wars than anything else in the history of creation."

Vocabulary

2 Babel (n.): the confusing sound of many voices talking together – **7 leech** (n.): /liːtʃ/ a small soft creature that fixes itself to the skin of animals in order to drink their blood – **9 carrier** (n.): something used for carrying something – **10 unconscious** (adj.): unable to see, move, feel, etc. in the normal way because you are not aware of it – **11 nourish** (v.): feed – **12 excrete** (v.) /ɪkˈskriːt/ (formal) to get rid of waste material from your body through your bowels, your skin, etc. – **13 telepathic matrix**: a living substance which sends out thoughts – **16 upshot** (n.): result

---

AWARENESS

1 Find out about efforts by language experts to establish a common language such as Esperanto. What other efforts have existed? Why have they all failed?

COMPREHENSION

2 How does the Babel fish work? Explain in your own words.
3 Why and how, according to the Bible's parable, does the attempt to build a huge tower fail?

ANALYSIS

4 Relate the Babel fish to the Tower of Babel.
5 Compare the results of using the Babel fish (in the science-fiction story) with those of giving people different languages (in the Bible).

OPINION

6 Why does the Babel fish cause wars and conflicts? Shouldn't it lead to better intergalactic understanding?
7 Why, on the contrary, do many languages cause conflicts in the parable in the Bible?
8 What is your opinion? Do different languages cause conflicts, and would a common language lead to more or less understanding and peace?

9 Find out more about Adams' cult science-fiction trilogy, which actually consists of five parts, on the internet. If you like science fiction and/or humorous books, you may also want to read parts of *The Hitchhiker's Guide to the Universe* such as *The Restaurant at the End of the Universe* or *Life, the Universe and Everything.* You may also want to view the film adaptation from 2005, *The Hitchhiker's Guide to the Galaxy.*

The Tower of Babel

The tower of Babel appears in a story in the Old Testament of the Bible (Gen. xi). According to the story, everyone originally spoke the same language, but when the people of Babel tried to build a tower that would reach to Heaven, God prevented them by making them all speak different languages. The people could not understand each other, and were unable to finish building the tower. People sometimes use the word "babel" to talk about a situation in which many people are talking at the same time and it is impossible to understand anyone.

Pieter Brueghel: The "Little" Tower of Babel *(c. 1563), Museum Boymans-van Benningen, Rotterdam, Oil on Board*

5

David Crystal

The Circle of World Englishes

One way of representing the unity and diversity of the English-speaking world is a visualization by means of the circle below. At the centre is placed the notion of World English, regarded as a 'common core'. Around it are placed the various regional or national standards, either establishing or becoming established. On the outside are examples of the wide range of popular Englishes which exist. From David Crystal, *The Cambridge Encyclopedia of the English Language* (2nd ed. Cambridge UP, 2004, 106).

Ban Ki-Moon (UN)

Mel Gibson (Australia)

Aishwarga Rai (India)

Queen Elizabeth II (UK)

Barack Obama (USA)

Jacob Zuma (South Africa)

Rihanna (Caribbean)

Michael Bublé (Canada)

WORLD STANDARD ENGLISH

East Asian Standardizing English

South Asian Standard(izing) English

West, East and South(ern) African Standard(izing) English

Caribbean Standard English

Australian, New Zealand & South Pacific Standard English

British and Irish Standard English

American Standard English

Canadian Standard English

AWARENESS

1 Think of situations where you have communicated in English with non-native speakers. How did you use English as a *lingua franca* (a language of international communication)?

COMPREHENSION

2 Compare all the graphs and texts on the spread of English on the preceding pages (chapters 2, 3).
3 Describe the varieties of English as shown in the survey above.
4 Try to find the states mentioned in the graph on this page on a map.

ANALYSIS

5   What is not included in the models presented here are factors like class and local dialect. Comment on their importance.

OPINION

6   What do you think of the idea of "international English" or "CNN English" or "Euroenglish"? Should they become acceptable forms of English, as more and more non-native speakers use English?

7   What sort of English are you learning? What sort of English would you like to learn and speak? Why?

PROJECT

8   English has also been called a "killer language". Find out about languages that are in danger of disappearing.

INTERNET PROJECTS

9   Search for sound archives on the internet where you can hear how English differs from region to region, from country to country. Useful sources are, for example, www.world-english.org and www.fonetiks.org.

10   Try to find more celebrities that you can match to the circle on p. 16.

Background Reading

Anyone really interested in the English language will find a wealth of material exploring the past, present and future status of the language in David Crystal's *The Cambridge Encyclopedia of the English Language*. Its first edition appeard in 1995; there have been numerous subsequent reprintings. The second edition, published with Cambridge University Press in 2004, includes updated texts, pictures, maps and graphics.

"Madam & Eve: 'Why Can't Everyone in This Country Speak Proper English?'"

George Bernard Shaw, a great playwright and essayist, once said about American and British English: "England and America are two countries divided by a common language." For students of English, the question has always been which of the two varieties they should learn. Recently, however, we have become aware of a multitude of "Englishes" existing all over the world – and they all demand to be treated equally. One is South African English. As we learn from the cartoon on page 18, in this country, too, there are some who put emphasis on 'correct' pronunciation and think that there is only one variety which should be privileged.

The South African cartoon strip "Madam & Eve" is immensely popular, not just in the country of its origin. It is read by over four million people worldwide. On the website www.madamandeve.co.za you can access a cartoon archive and look at the cartoon of the day. The cartoons take a humorous look at the daily lives of two people from different backgrounds as they experience life in post-apartheid South Africa. There is Madam, a South African lady, who is used to a posh and upper-class lifestyle and is struggling to come to terms with the new South Africa. Then there is her smart and sometimes not-so-obedient servant Eve. In the cartoon on page 18, Madam's mother, who is from England, finds fault with the newsreader's pronunciation, while Eve and another servant couldn't care less.

Info

Background

The cartoon is based on a famous song by Louis Armstrong and Ella Fitzgerald, composed by George and Ira Gershwin, "Let's Call the Whole Thing Off", from 1937. The song is about the differences between British and American English. Here are some lines from it:

You say eether and I say eyether,
You say neether and I say nyther;
Eether, eyether, neether, nyther –
Let's call the whole thing off!

You like potato and I like po-tah-to,
You like tomato and I like to-mah-to;
Potato, po-tah-to, tomato, to-mah-to –
Let's call the whole thing off!

Vocabulary

(First picture) **commission** (v.): formally ask someone to write an official report – (fourth picture) **call off** (v.): decide that s.th. should be stopped after it has already started – (fifth to seventh picture) **Kwaito / Durban**: names of cities in South Africa

TASKS

1 Read the cartoon and song aloud. Try to make differences in pronunciation.
2 Try to characterize the persons in the cartoon. What does it say about language and class?
3 What makes the cartoon funny?
4 How does the cartoon relate to the original song's lines?
5 What is the message, both of the song and the cartoon?

6

Thomas L. Friedman

"The Five Gas Stations of the World"

The journalist Thomas L. Friedman was born in Minneapolis in 1953, educated at Brandeis University and St. Anthony's College, Oxford. For his first book, *From Beirut to Jerusalem*, he was awarded the National Book Award in the US. He has also won two prestigious Pulitzer Prizes for reporting for *The New York Times*. Living in Bethesda, Maryland, he is today one of the most prominent supporters of globalization. His main publication on the issue is the book *The Lexus and the Olive Tree*. In its title, the contradictions of the age of globalization are symbolized. The Lexus, a large, high-tech luxury car made by the "global player" Toyota, is one aspect of this process; the olive tree as the product of traditional farming and production methods is its complementary symbol. – Thomas L. Friedman, *The Lexus and the Olive Tree: Understanding Globalization* (New York: Anchor Books, 2000), 379–381.

1 I believe in the five gas stations theory of the world. That's right: I believe you can reduce the world's economies today to basically five different gas stations. First there is the Japanese gas station. Gas is $5 a gallon.
5 Four men in uniforms and white gloves, with lifetime employment contracts, wait on you. They pump your gas. They change your oil. They wash your windows, and they wave at you with a friendly smile as you drive away in peace. Second is the American gas station. Gas
10 costs only $1 a gallon, but you pump it yourself. You wash your own windows. You fill your own tires. And when you drive around the corner four homeless people try to steal your hubcaps. Third is the Western European gas station. Gas there also costs $5 a gallon. There is
15 only one man on duty. He grudgingly pumps your gas and unsmilingly changes your oil, reminding you all the time that his union contract says he only has to pump gas and change oil. He doesn't do windows. He works only thirty-five hours a week, with ninety min-
20 utes off each day for lunch, during which time the gas station is closed. He also has six weeks' vacation every summer in the south of France. Across the street, his two brothers and uncle, who have not worked in ten years because their state unemployment insurance pays
25 more than their last job, are playing boccie ball. Fourth is the developing-country gas station. Fifteen people work there and they are all cousins. When you drive in, no one pays any attention to you because they all are busy talking to each other. Gas is only 35 cents a gallon
30 because it is subsidized by the government, but only one of the six gas pumps actually works. The others are broken and they are waiting for the replacement parts to be flown in from Europe. The gas station is rather run-down because the absentee owner lives in Zurich and
35 takes all the profits out of the country. The owner doesn't know that half his employees actually sleep in the repair shop at night and use the car wash equipment to shower. Most of the customers at the developing-country gas station either drive the latest-model Mercedes or a motor scooter – nothing in between. The
40 place is always busy, though, because so many people stop in to use the air pump to fill their bicycle tires. Lastly there is the communist gas station. Gas there is only 50 cents a gallon – but there is none, because the four guys working there have sold it all on the black
45 market for $5 a gallon. Just one of the four guys who is employed at the communist gas station is actually there. The other three are working at second jobs in the underground economy and only come around once a week to collect their paychecks.
50

What is going on in the world today, in the very broadest sense, is that through the process of globalization everyone is being forced toward America's gas station. If you are not an American and don't know how to pump your own gas, I suggest you learn. With
55 the end of the Cold War, globalization is globalizing Anglo-American-style capitalism and the Golden Straitjacket. It is globalizing American culture and cultural icons. It is globalizing the best of America and the worst of America. It is globalizing the American Revo-
60 lution and it is globalizing the American gas station.

But not everyone likes the American gas station and what it stands for, and you can understand why. Embedded in the Japanese, Western European and communist gas stations are social contracts very different from the
65 American one, as well as very different attitudes about how markets should operate and be controlled. The Europeans and the Japanese believe in the state exercising power over the people and over markets, while Americans tend to believe more in empowering the people and let-
70 ting markets be as free as possible to sort out who wins and who loses.

Because the Japanese, Western Europeans and communists are uncomfortable with totally unfettered markets and the unequal benefits and punishments they distribute, their gas stations are designed to cushion such inequalities and to equalize rewards. Their gas stations also pay more attention to the distinctive traditions and value preferences of their communities. The Western Europeans do this by employing fewer people, but paying them higher wages and collecting higher taxes to generously support the unemployed and to underwrite a goody bag of other welfare-state handouts. The Japanese do it by paying people a little less but guaranteeing them a lifetime employment, and then protecting those lifetime jobs and benefits by restricting foreign competitors from entering the Japanese market. The American gas station, by contrast, is a much more efficient place to drive through: the customer is the

king; the gas station has no social function; its only purpose is to provide the most gas at the cheapest price. If that can be done with no employees at all – well, all the better. A flexible labor market will find them work somewhere else. Too cruel, you say? Maybe so. But, ready or not, this is the model that the rest of the world is increasingly being pressured to emulate.

Vocabulary

4 gallon (n.): a unit for measuring liquids, equal to eight pints; in the US it is 3.79 litres – **5 lifetime employment contract**: a written statement by the state or a company granting you a job for life – **13 hubcap** (n.): a round metal cover for the centre of a wheel on a vehicle – **15 grudgingly** (adv.): showing a feeling of dislike – **17 union contract**: official agreement with an organization representing workers – **24 state unemployment insurance**: money you get from the state when you are out of work – **25 boccie ball**: a game similar to lawn bowling played on a long narrow usually dirt court – **30 subsidize** (v.): the government pays part of the cost of a company – **34 absentee owner**: the owner is somewhere else – **63**

embedded (adj.): to be put firmly and deeply into something – **77 unfettered** (adj.): /ʌnˈfetəd/ not restricted by laws or rules – **81 cushion** (v.): to protect someone from an unpleasant situation – **83 reward** (n.): something that you get because you have done something good or helpful or have worked hard – **83 equalize rewards**: give the same reward to everybody – **95 underwrite** (v.): here: support s. th. with money – **96 goody bag**: something which is full of pleasant and desirable things – **106 labor market**: the people looking for work and the jobs that are available at that time – **109 emulate** (v.): /ˈemjuleɪt/ do something or behave in the same way as someone else, especially because you admire them

Explanation

57 Golden Straitjacket: a central metaphor used by Friedman for the condition most economically advanced states are in. The usual image is that of a golden cage (straitjacket: AE; BE: straightjacket: /ˈstreɪtˌdʒæk·ɪt/ 1. a special piece of clothing that prevents someone from moving their arms,

used to control someone who is being violent or, in the past, someone who was mentally ill. 2. something such as a law or set of ideas that puts very strict or unfair limits on someone)

Awareness

1 How do attitudes towards work and the economy differ worldwide? Remember impressions you gained when abroad. Also think about some of the clichés that exist about the work ethic in other countries.

2 What is the common image of American, African, Asian, etc. attitudes towards work?

3 How does the process of globalization influence work, especially job perspectives, in your country?

4 Think of globalization as a process of many conflicts and contradictions. Friedman uses the pair of the Lexus and the olive tree. Make a list of similar contradictory couples that could symbolize the global village.

Comprehension

5 Divide the text into sections.

6 Look at the first part of the text dealing with the five gas stations. Describe in your own words the particularities of each station. How do the gas stations reflect on the countries' respective mentality?

7 What, according to the text, becomes clear about the differences between the world economies?

8 Make a list of all the negative sides of non-American gas stations as mentioned in the text, beginning with lifetime employment contracts, state subsidies, etc.

9 Then make a list of all the positive aspects of American gas stations.

10 Why, according to the author, is the American gas station possibly the only solution to the world's problems?

11 Look at the last part of the text. What are the conclusions the author draws from his comparisons? Do you agree?

Analysis

12 Comment on the author's description of the gas stations. What peculiarities does he choose in each case and why? Does he exaggerate? If yes, is there some truth in his descriptions?

13 Comment in detail on the author's summing up of the disadvantages of non-American gas stations and the recipe he offers to the rest of the world.

14 Why are more and more countries "pressured" to follow the American model? Give some suggestions.

15 Explain the "Golden Straitjacket" image.

16 Explain the term "lifetime employment contract" and comment on its usage in the text (ll. 5f.). What, on the contrary, is meant and implied by the term "flexible labor market" (l. 105)?

17 Why, according to the author, are state subsidies negative for the economy?

18 Why is the term "efficiency" so important in the context of globalization? Give some suggestions.

Opinion

19 "The customer is king" – discuss this term, referring to experiences in your own country.

20 What consequences might follow if we all were to imitate the model of the American gas station?

21 Comment on the author's pro-American attitude.

22 Why does globalization equal Americanization for many people?

23 Do you think that Americanization has its advantages?

24 To what degree has everyday life in your country become Americanized?

Projects

25 Read more passages from *The Lexus and the Olive Tree* or *The World is Flat* (2005). Both books offer a wealth of information on what effects globalization has on everyday lives everywhere on this planet. Write a book review, commenting on Friedman's optimistic view on globalization as Americanization (you may want to consult other articles on both books first).

26 Imagine being a politician who has to introduce a new economic model, less social than the existing one because of severe cuts to adapt to the international market situation. Make a list of the arguments which might come up in favour of or against this model.

27 The American gas station, according to Friedman, has "no social function; its only purpose is to provide". What do you know about the economic system in your country? Which implications does its concept have? Is it a good idea to abandon it completely in favour of an American-style economy as described by Friedman?

7 "10 International Fallacies"

Translation often proves to be a difficult task. Translating cultures or cultural products is even more difficult. Here is an (absolutely incomplete) list of "international fallacies" – global marketing mistakes by global companies. – A similar list was first published in the *Sarasota Herald Tribune*, January 19, 1998.

1. Pepsi's "Come alive with the Pepsi Generation" was translated into Chinese as "Pepsi brings your ancestors back from the grave".
2. Frank Perdue's chicken slogan "It takes a strong man to make a tender chicken" was translated into Spanish as "It takes an aroused man to make a chicken affectionate".
3. The Coca-Cola name in China was first read as "Ke-kou-ke-la", meaning "Bite the wax tadpole". Coke then researched 40,000 characters to find a phonetic equivalent, "ko-kou-ko-le", translating into "happiness in the mouth".
4. When Gillette marketed a ballpoint pen in Mexico, the ads were supposed to have read, "It won't leak in your pocket and embarrass you". Instead, mistranslation resulted in the ad reading, "It won't leak in your pocket and make you pregnant".
5. In Puerto Rico, the Chevrolet Nova was accepted only hesitantly due to its name ("no va" = "does not drive"). In the end, its name had to be changed completely.
6. Nike wasted an undisclosed sum of money by having its products in Europe endorsed by the baseball and football star Bo Jackson – who, unfortunately, was completely unknown there.
7. Mac Donnel Douglas had to revoke brochures from the Indian market, having discovered that the persons displayed were not Indian but Pakistani.
8. Due to the fact that newspapers are read from right to left in Arabic countries, some readers there were puzzled about a print advertisement which showed clean laundry being treated with detergent and coming out of the laundromat stained.
9. For the World Cup in 1994, McDonald's and Coca-Cola had the Saudi Arabian flag printed on soda cans and paper bags. Unfortunately, they failed to realize that the flag contains the phrase "There is no God except Allah, and Mohammed is his prophet". The use of this phrase for advertising purposes and the fact that most cans and paper bags end up on the floor and are trampled on were unacceptable to devout Muslims.
10. In Japanese, the trade name "Esso" means "a car which has broken down".

Vocabulary

fallacy (n.): /ˈfæləsɪ/ misconception, a false idea or belief, especially one that a lot of people believe is true – **6 arouse** (v.): excite sexually – **7 affectionate** (adj.): loving, caring – **9 tadpole** (n.): a small creature that has a long tail, lives in water, and grows into a frog or toad – **15 em-** **barrass** (v.): make s.o. feel ashamed, nervous, or uncomfortable – **23 endorse** (v.): if a famous person endorses a product or service, they say in an advertisement that they use and like it – **42 devout** (adj.): /dɪˈvaʊt/ s.o. who is devout has a very strong belief in a religion

AWARENESS

1 Make a list of products which have a different name in other countries – remember your holidays or other times abroad. Why do companies use different names for the same product?

COMPREHENSION

2 Explain in a few words why the products did not sell.

ANALYSIS

3 Point out the cases of cross-cultural misunderstandings which are based on language problems. Describe in each case how two languages interfere, that is "collide".

4 Find the cases which are based on problems with culturally different values, norms and attitudes. Explain what these incidents reveal about different value systems.

COMMENT

5 How could cross-cultural mistakes as described here be avoided? Suggest some solutions.

6 Linguistically, a typical source of mistakes are "false friends" such as "gift" or "actually" – which do not mean the same in other languages. Can you think of some other false friends? Make a list.

8

Anup Shah

"Global Financial Crisis"

Anup Shah, born 1974 and grown up in England, is the editor and publicist of the website www.globalissues.org. Starting off in 1998 as a privately funded page maintained during spare-time, it has now become a full time project. The article below tries to give a dense overview about the facts and coherences as well as a prospect of the global financial crisis, which started in 2008. – Anup Shah, "Global Financial Crisis", 11 December 2010, online <http://www.globalissues.org/issue/38/free-trade-and-globalization>.

1 Following a period of economic boom, a financial bubble – global in scope – has now burst. The extent of this problem has been so severe that some of the world's largest financial institutions have collapsed.
5 Others have been bought out by their competition at low prices and in other cases, the governments of the wealthiest nations in the world have resorted to extensive bail-out and rescue packages for the remaining large banks and financial institutions.

10 Some of the bail-outs have also led to charges of hypocrisy due to the apparent socializing of the costs while privatizing the profits. Furthermore, the institutions being rescued are typically the ones that got the world into this trouble in the first place. For smaller
15 businesses and poorer people, such options for bail-out and rescue are rarely available when they find themselves in crisis. There is the argument that when the larger banks show signs of crisis, it is not just the wealthy that will suffer, but potentially everyone
20 because of the ripple effect that problems at the top could have throughout the entire economy.

Plummeting stock markets have wiped out 33% of the value of companies, $14.5 trillion. Taxpayers will be bailing out their banks and financial institutions with large amounts of money. US taxpayers alone will 25 spend some $9.7 trillion in bail-out packages and plans. The UK and other European countries have also spent some $2 trillion on rescues and bail-out packages. More is expected. Much more.

Such numbers, made quickly available, are enough 30 to wipe many individual's mortgages, or clear out third world debt many times over. Even the high military spending figures are dwarfed by the bailout plans to date.

This problem could have been averted (in theory) as 35 people had been pointing to these issues for decades. However, during boom, very few want to hear such pessimism. Does this crisis spell an end to the careless forms of banking and finance and will it herald a better economic age, or are we just doomed to keep forget- 40 ting history and repeat these mistakes in the future? Signs are not encouraging as rich nations are resisting meaningful reform …

Vocabulary

2 scope (n.): the range of things that a subject, activity, book etc deals with – **2 burst** (v.): if s.th. bursts or if you burst it, it breaks open or apart suddenly and violently so that its contents come out – **2 extent** (n.): how large, important, or serious s.th. is, especially s.th. such as a problem or injury – **3 severe** (adj.): very bad or very serious – **5 competition** (n.): the people or the groups that are competing against you, especially in business or in a sport – **8 bail-out** (n.): (informal) financial help given to a person or a company that is in difficulty – **10 charge** (n.): a written or spoken statement blaming someone for doing s.th. bad or illegal – **11 hypocrisy** (n.): when someone pretends to have certain beliefs or opinions that they do not really have, used to show disapproval – **11 apparent** (adj.): easy

to notice – **16 available** (adj.): s.th. that is able to be used or can easily be bought or found – **20 ripple effect** (n.): a situation in which one action causes another, which then causes a third etc (= domino effect) – **22 plummeting** (v.): to suddenly and quickly decrease in value or amount – **22 wipe out** (v.): to destroy, remove, or get rid of s.th. completely – **32 debt** (n.): a sum of money that a person or organization owes – **33 dwarf** (v.): to be so big that other things are made to seem small – **39 herald** (v.): to be a sign of s.th. that is going to come or happen soon – **40 doomed to** (v.): to make someone or s.th. certain to fail, die, be destroyed etc – **42 resist** (v.): to try to prevent a change from happening, or prevent yourself from being forced to do

Awareness

1 What do you know about the recent financial crisis?
2 Do you feel affected by economic problems in Europe or world-wide?

Comprehension

3 Sum up the reasons for the financial and economic crisis stated by the author.
4 According to the author, are there signs that this crisis can be solved?

Analysis

5 Assign a number of key words to each paragraph.
6 Then analyse how the author develops his arguments in this article.
7 What does the author write about the role of banks?

Opinion

8 What is your opinion on how banks should be treated financially?
9 Discuss other ways of coping with the financial and economic crisis.

Internet Project

10 Find out more about the recent crisis by consulting the websites of some international newspapers.

The bull on Wall Street – a symbol of rising markets and of capitalism

Definitions

Info

WTO: The World Trade Organization, an international organization, established in 1995 and based in Geneva, that deals with the rules of trade between different nations, and encourages them to trade in a fair manner.

WB: The World Bank, an organization that is part of the UN (United Nations), which lends money to poorer countries so that they can develop their farming, industry, and health and education systems. Its official name is the International Bank for Reconstruction and Development.

UN: United Nations, an international organization that tries to find peaceful solutions to world problems.

IMF: The International Monetary Fund, an international organization that tries to encourage trade between countries and to help poorer countries develop economically.

Naomi Klein

9

No Logo

Naomi Klein, born in Canada in 1970, is a Toronto-based journalist and regular television commentator. She is one of the most prominent opponents of globalization, which she views as a disastrous process for the individual, especially in developing countries. For her, multinational corporations are to be blamed for worldwide exploitation and degradation, child labour and work in sweat shops (underpaid jobs under primitive conditions). She voices her opinions in contributions to newspapers such as Canada's leading quality daily, *The Toronto Globe & Mail*. Her column has recently been syndicated worldwide in the British newspaper *The Guardian*. Her book *No Logo* has been translated into many languages, and its title has become a veritable slogan for all those attacking the power of multinational corporations. The following passage from *No Logo* first describes her general attitude towards the multinationals; in the second part (from l. 35) there is an instance of exploitation of workers in the industrial zone of Cavite near Rosario on the Philippines. – Naomi Klein, *No Logo* (New York: Picador, 2000), xvii, 203f.

1 Usually, reports about this global web of logos and products are couched in the euphoric marketing rhetoric of the global village, an incredible place, where tribespeople in remotest rain forests tap away on laptop
5 computers, Sicilian grandmothers conduct E-business, and "global teens" share, to borrow a phrase from a Levi's Web site, "a world-wide style culture". Everyone from Coke to McDonald's to Motorola has tailored their marketing strategy around this post-national vision,
10 but it is IBM's long-running "Solutions for a Small Planet" campaign that most eloquently captures the equalizing promise of the logo-linked globe. [...]

This is a village where some multinationals, far from leveling the global playing field with jobs and technol-
15 ogy for all, are in the process of mining the planet's poorest back country for unimaginable profits. This is the village where Bill Gates lives, amassing a fortune of $ 55 billion while a third of his workforce is classified as temporary workers, and where competitors are
20 either incorporated into the Microsoft monolith or made obsolete by the latest feat in software bundling. This is the village where we are indeed connected to one another through a web of brands, but the underside of that web reveals designer slums like the one I visited
25 outside Jakarta. IBM claims that its technology spans the globe, and so it does, but often its international presence takes the form of cheap Third World labor producing the computer chips and power sources that drive our machines. On the outskirts of Manila, for in-
30 stance, I met a seventeen-year old girl who assembles CD-ROM drives for IBM. I told her I was impressed that someone so young could do such high-tech work. "We make computers," she told me, "but we don't know how to operate computers." Ours, it would seem, is not such a small planet after all. [...]
35

Windowless workshops made of cheap plastic and aluminium siding are crammed in next to each other, only feet apart. Racks of time cards bake in the sun, making sure the maximum amount of work is extracted from each worker, the maximum number of working
40 hours extracted from each day. The streets in the zone are eerily empty, and open doors – the ventilation system for most factories – reveal lines of young women hunched in silence over clamoring machines.

In other parts of the world, workers live inside the
45 economic zones, but not in Cavite: this is a place of pure work. All the bustle and color of Rosario abruptly stops at the gates, where workers must show their ID cards to armed guards in order to get inside. Visitors are rarely permitted. [...]
50

Inside the gates, factory workers assemble the finished products of our branded world: Nike running shoes, Gap pajamas, IBM computer screens, Old Navy jeans. But [...] [t]heir names and logos aren't splashed on the façades of the factories in the industrial zone.
55

Vocabulary

1 logo (n.): a small design that is the official sign of a company or organization – **2 couch** (v.): (formal) to be expressed in a particular way – **2 euphoric marketing rhetoric:** very optimistic usage of language in favour of the market – **4 remotest** (adj.): very remote, far away – **5 conduct** (v.): do, perform – **11 eloquently** (adv.): expressing ideas and plans well – **11 capture** (v.): catch – **12 equalize** (v.): to make two or more things the same in size, value, amount etc. – **15 mine** (v.): (here) search and remove – **18 classify** (v.): to regard people or things as belonging to a particular group because they have similar qualities – **19 competitor** (n.): rival – **20 incorporate** (v.): make part of – **20 monolith** (n.): a large, powerful organization that cannot change quickly – **21 obsolete** (adj.): no longer useful – **21 feat in software bundling:** progress or trick in providing computer software and sometimes other equipment or services that are included with a new computer at no extra cost – **25 span** (v.): to include the whole of it – **29 Manila:** capital of the Philippines – **30 assemble** (v.): put together – **36 workshop** (n.): a room or building where tools and machines are used for making or repairing things – **37 siding** (n.): (AE) long, narrow pieces of wood, metal, or plastic, used for covering the outside walls of houses – **37 crammed in** (v.): squeezed in – **38 rack** (n.): a frame or shelf that has bars or hooks on which you can put things – **38 time card:** a piece of card on which the hours you have worked are recorded by a special machine – **41 extract** (v.): to remove from, get from (p. p.) – **42 eerie** (adj.): /ˈɪərɪ/ strange and frightening – **44 hunched:** bent over – **44 clamor** (v.): make a loud noise – **52 branded** (adj.): (ambivalent usage) belonging to a brand, (past participle) burn a mark onto something – **54 splash** (v.): to make someone or something wet with a lot of small drops of water or other liquid; here: to display

AWARENESS

1 Do you prefer clothes and shoes with brand names? Why/why not?
2 Look at the labels of your clothes. Where were they produced? What do you know about working conditions there?

COMPREHENSION

3 What, exactly, is the "promise of the logo-linked globe" (l. 12)?
4 Write down the points Klein makes about the darker sides of the global village.
5 Why are the working conditions described here inhuman? In your answer, refer to the second part of the excerpt.

ANALYSIS

6 Give instances of the "market rhetoric" Klein critizises in the first paragraph. How does this rhetoric work? How does Klein reveal its ideology?
7 In the second paragraph (beginning with l. 13), Klein uses a simple, but very effective stylistic device. Name it and describe its effects on the reader.
8 What is meant by the last sentence of the second paragraph, "Ours, it would seem, is not such a small planet after all"?
9 What is the effect the author wants to achieve with her description of working conditions in a workshop in Cavite? How does she achieve this effect?

OPINION

10 In the first paragraph, Klein mentions the "post-national vision" of the multinationals. What, to your opinion, is this vision? What would a world without national barriers look like? Is this positive or negative?
11 What could be done to improve working conditions in developing countries?

PROJECT

12 Read *No Logo* and write a book report. Or find out about Naomi Klein on the internet. Present your findings to your group/class. Discuss Klein's opinion. Why has she become a popular representative of anti-globalization forces?

10 | "My Name Is Amanda"

On the internet, organizations try to raise awareness about the job conditions of workers in developing countries. On this page, you can see two pictures depicting working conditions in so-called 'sweat shops'. The statement by Amanda is an authentic statement (source: www.cleanclothes.org).

1 My name is Amanda, I am 20 years old. I work in a garment factory in Jakarta, Indonesia. I sew Levi's jeans. Though I have to work 75 hours a week, I am making less than minimum wage. Even the minimum
5 wage would not be enough to live on. I can barely buy food with what I make. We cannot refuse to do overtime, they fire you. One time we went on strike to demand better wages and a transportation and food allowance. The management refused to give in to our
10 demands and the people who were suspected to have organized the strike were fired.

Vocabulary

2 garment (n.): clothes – **2 sew** (v.): /səʊ/ use a needle and thread to make or repair clothes or to fasten something such as a button to them – **4 minimum wage:** the lowest amount of money that an employer can legally pay to a worker – **8 food allowance:** money you get for buying food – **9 give in to our demands:** finally do what we expected them to do – **10 suspect** (v.): think that s.o. is probably guilty of s.th.

TASK

1 Compare the pictures and the text. Describe what they tell you about working conditions in developing countries. Explain how the text and the pictures affect you as a western consumer.

PROJECTS

2 Find out more about working conditions in developing countries on the internet. For example, use www.cleanclothes.org.

3 Get information about ATTAC, a global network including trade unions and non-governmental organizations, which tries "to prevent further deprivation of workers' rights worldwide".
Discuss with other members of your class whether you would support ATTAC or not.

11

Michael Veseth

"Nike and the Global Swoosh"

The sportswear company Nike is one of the truly global players, whose well-known trademark, the Swoosh, has become an icon of the sports world and leisure industry. In the following text, the author Michael Veseth looks at some of the reasons behind Nike's international success story. – Michael Veseth, *Selling Globalization: The Myth of the Global Economy* (Boulder/London: Lynne Rienner Publishers, 1998), 50–52.

1 Throughout its history, Nike has consistently combined technical innovation and aggressive marketing. Its
5 business still includes running shoes but now includes a wide range of other products in both footwear and sports-related markets. I have not
10 yet seen a Nike perfume or cologne, but it would not surprise me if one exists. Nike's trademark is that well known. [...]

15 Nike is truly global by my definition because it swims in both pools. It has helped create a global consumption pool for its sports-related products, which it makes by drawing resources from the global production pool. It works hard at making both production and con-
20 sumption global, reaps enormous profits, and takes a good deal of criticism in the process.

Nike does not have many employees (only about 14,000 in 1995) for a corporation with almost $ 5 billion in sales (1995) and a market value of nearly $ 10 billion
25 (1995). The key to this high productivity is that Nike's core business employees do not make shoes: Their job is to make customers. To do this, they make images and icons. Shoes, I think, are almost an afterthought. Nike invests heavily in creating demand for its prod-
30 ucts by building its stable of celebrity endorsers and making the swoosh a symbol of their lifestyles. [...]

Nike's success at creating a global trademark makes it vulnerable to charges of cultural imperialism by people who argue that globalization is the end of culture.

Nike does not own the factories that make its shoes. 35 It typically forms partnerships with local firms or with Korean or Taiwanese investors. Nike pays wages that are usually high by local standards. In Indonesia, for example, factory wages of $ 2.28 per day are both legal (the national minimum wage is $ 2.28) and high 40 enough to attract 120,000 workers to factory jobs making Nike shoes because so many other jobs do not pay even this legal minimum wage. (The Nike-contracted factories in Indonesia therefore employ almost 100 times as many workers as Nike itself!) [...] 45

"Whether you like Nike or don't like Nike, good corporations are the ones that lead these countries out of poverty", said Nike Chairman Philip Knight in an interview. "When we started in Japan, factory labor there was making $ 4 a day, which is basically what is 50 being paid in Indonesia and being so strongly criticized today. Nobody today is saying, 'The poor old Japanese.' We watched it happen all over again in Taiwan and Korea, and now it's going on in Southeast Asia."

Vocabulary

swoosh (n.): Nike's trademark, often used without the company's name; (v.) making a sound by moving quickly through the air - **2 consistent** (adj.): continuing to happen or develop in the same way - **7 range** (n.): a set of similar products made by a particular company - **18 drawing resources**: using what is available to the company - **20 reap** (v.): get as a result of what they have done - **26 core business**: main business - **28 afterthought** (n.): something that you mention or add later because you did not think of it or plan it before - **30 celebrity endorsers**: a famous person saying in an advertisement that they use and like a product or service - **33 charge** (n.): accusation - **43 Nike-contracted** (adj.): companies have signed a contract in which they agree formally that they will produce for the company

AWARENESS

1 What image do brand names project?

COMPREHENSION

2 What points are made about the reasons of Nike's success?
3 Why is Nike "truly global"?
4 What is Nike's business philosophy?
5 Why, according to Nike's Chairman, does Nike lead developing countries out of poverty?

ANALYSIS

6 Is the author of this article in favour of or against Nike's business policy? Give reasons for your opinion.
7 What is implied by the expression that Nike "swims in both pools"?
8 What are "sports-related markets" and what is their importance for a company?
9 Describe the reasons for Nike's success, referring to expressions like "images and icons", "celebrity endorsers" and "lifestyles".
10 What makes Nike vulnerable to charges of "cultural imperialism"?
11 What comparisons are drawn between Japan and (the rest of) Asia? Can such comparisons be made?

OPINION

12 Discuss "labour justice" in the context of sweat shops and the fact that wages by multinationals are above local average.
13 Does Nike improve the standard of living and working conditions in the countries in which it contracts its factories?
14 Do you think that Nike's recipe for success is followed by more companies?
15 Is Nike a typical example of worldwide contracting? What do you know about other companies such as Adidas, Puma, Asics, etc.?

INTERNET PROJECT

16 Find out more about the power of international corporations by consulting the following websites. Discuss the pros and cons of big companies like Nike. Should you change your behaviour as a consumer?

www.nologo.org
www.attac.org
www.adbusters.org
www.corporatewatch.org
www.citizen.org/trade/
www.hrw.org/
www.jwj.org/
www.wtowatch.org/

"Sorry lads. I'm closing this workshop down, and relocating in the far east."

GENERAL TASKS

17 Define "global capitalism".
18 Why is it seen as something negative? Who is being disadvantaged or exploited?
19 Are there alternatives to capitalism?

TASK REFERRING TO CARTOON

20 Explain the message of the cartoon and find recent examples from your own area.

The Environment

Whether we like it or not, we all contribute to environmental damage. The following article from *The New York Times* describes what some companies do to make consumers feel less guilty. – Harry Rijnen, "Offsetting Environmental Damage by Planes", *The New York Times*, 18 February 2003.

1 Do you feel guilty about global warming every time you get behind the wheel of your car? If you are a frequent flier, start feeling more guilty.

On a round trip from New York to London, according 5 to the calculations of the Edinburgh Centre for Carbon Management in Scotland, a Boeing 747 spews out about 440 tons of carbon dioxide, the main greenhouse gas. That is about the same amount that 80 S.U.V.'s emit in a full year of hard driving.

10 But short of swimming to London or jogging to Los Angeles, what is the concerned business traveler to do? The airline industry, busy trying to avoid bankruptcy, is not offering tips on how to limit the environmental damage. And chances are your travel agent has not given the matter much thought. [...] 15

Jonathan Shopley, Future Forests' chief executive, says his appeals to the airline industry have fallen on deaf ears. "They act towards this environmental problem like the chemical industry 20 years ago: If we ignore it, maybe it will go away," he said. "But it won't." [...] 20

The American software company Interface pays American Forests to plant a tree every 1,500 passenger miles its employees fly. "It's part of our program to minimize our impact on the environment," said Ray C. Anderson, Interface's chairman. "The cost is minimal, 25 and we create enormous good will."

Global warming – caused by burning oil, coal and gas – is the biggest environmental problem we face today

"The Prestige is Bahamas flagged, American classed, Greek owned by a company that may or may not be registered in Liberia, and chartered by a business that could be Russian or Swiss. Nobody yet knows."

Flood catastrophe in Europe

Oil tanker sinks off Spanish coast

Tsunami hits Asia

Vocabulary

6 spew out (v.): /spjuː/ make something flow out in large quantities – **7 carbon dioxide** (n.): the gas produced when animals breathe out, when carbon is burned in air, or when animal or vegetable substances decay – **8 S.U.V.**: sport-utility vehicle, a type of vehicle that is bigger than a car and is made for travelling over rough ground – **9 emit** (v.): send out – **11 concerned** (adj.): worried or involved – **17 fall on deaf ears**: those talked to do not listen – **24 impact** (n.): effect or influence – **25 chairman** (n.): someone, especially a man, who is in charge of a meeting or directs the work of a committee or an organization; today the expression "chairperson" is frequently used – **26 create good will**: to show that you care by a gesture

Explanations

5 Edinburgh Centre for Carbon Management in Scotland: an organization which controls pollution to the environment due to carbon dioxide emissions – **22 American Forests**: a non-profit organization which attempts to preserve forests in the USA – **cartoon: Des. Res.** (jargon): a desirable residence (an attractive home)

Vocabulary Collage

drought (n.): /draʊt/ a long period of dry weather when there is not enough water for plants and animals to live – **classed** (v.): (pp.) officially considered to belong to – **charter** (v.): to pay a company for the use of their aircraft, boat, etc. – **executive** (n.): manager

Overfishing hits industry and ecology

Droughts, floods, storms, melting ice caps, dying coral reefs

Executive Des.Res.
(ARCHITECT-DESIGNED FOR GLOBAL WARMING)

AWNING TO COUNTER EFFECTS OF OZONE HOLES

BOAT FOR HANDY SHOPPING TRIPS

ELECTRIC FENCE TO DETER ENVIRONMENTAL REFUGEES

ROOF RESERVOIR TO INSURE AGAINST DROUGHT

ANTI-POLLUTION FILTRATION AND AIR-CONDITIONING UNITS

TICKETS FOR INTERPLANETARY TRAVEL (IN SAFE)

HYDRAULIC RAMS TO PROTECT AGAINST RISING SEA LEVELS

Info

Global Warming

The **greenhouse effect** is a warming of the Earth's surface and lower atmosphere that tends to intensify with an increase in atmospheric carbon dioxide. A growing number of scientists estimate that global average temperatures could increase by as much as 5 °C (9 °F) by the middle of the 21st century.

Global warming is the phenomenon in which the density in the atmosphere of gases such as carbon dioxide rises and in turn causes the air temperature to rise. Forests are where carbon is accumulated in large amounts from the atmosphere through photosynthesis. When trees are felled and burned carbon dioxide is released, and even if the felled trees are left where they're chopped, they will eventually release carbon dioxide. The reduction of forests is thus also a primary factor of global warming.

The **ozone layer** is that part of the stratosphere which contains ozone. Ozone is notable for its ability to absorb certain frequencies of ultraviolet radiation. The ozone layer is not very dense; if it were compressed to the density of the troposphere, it would be only a few millimeters thick. (Compiled from various internet sources.)

AWARENESS

1 Look carefully at the collage on pages 30–31. All the headlines and texts are from newspapers. Describe what environmental problems they refer to.

2 Are there further environmental problems which are not referred to in the collage? Look at recent newspaper headlines and try to make a list.

COMPREHENSION

3 What is so disturbing about the oil catastrophe caused by the sinking of the Prestige off the coast of Spain in 2002?

4 Link this disaster to other oil spills caused by oil tankers over the last year. What is the pattern, which is also hinted at in the quote about the Prestige?

5 Describe the irony in the two cartoons of the collage and this page.

6 According to the newspaper article, why does flying cause so much damage to the environment?

7 Why is the airline industry not really concerned?

8 Describe what an American software company does to help the environment.

ANALYSIS

9 How does the beginning of the newspaper article create a feeling of guilt in its reader?

10 What exactly is implied by the comparison of the airline industry with the chemical industry twenty years ago?

11 What is meant by "creating good will" in this context?

OPINION

12 What is your opinion on the American software company's approach to the problem of environmental pollution?

13 Consider some other steps companies could take to do something for the environment. Make a list.

INTERNET PROJECT

14 Consult the English website of Greenpeace. Greenpeace is an international organization whose members work actively to protect the environment from damage caused by industrial processes or military activities. It uses its own boats to try to prevent governments from testing nuclear weapons and other sea animals from being killed. Then discuss whether you agree with Greenpeace's policy (www.greenpeace.org).

"Your Aerosol Affects the Life of a Goat Herder in Mongolia"

BY S.FRANCIS, H.DUGMORE & RICO

I'M TELLING THE TRUTH! SPRAYING AEROSOL DEODORANTS AFFECTS THE PLANET'S OZONE LAYER

HOW YOU TREAT YOUR UNDERARMS HERE ... CAN AFFECT GOAT HERDERS IN MONGOLIA.

THAT'S RIDICUCOUS.

MONGOLIA

ШНИСИ ДАШНОС ARMPITS ОСНСРШЧ EDITH ANDERSON.

Vocabulary

aerosol (n.): /ˈeərəsɒl/ a small metal container with liquid inside. You press a button on the container to make the liquid come out in very small drops - **affect** (v.) /əˈfekt/ to do something that produces an effect or change in something or in someone's situation - **goat** (n.) an animal that has horns on top of its head and long hair under its chin, and can climb steep hills and rocks - **Mongolia**: a country in north central Asia between Russia and China. Mongolia is a large country but has a small population because it includes a large area of desert and open plains - **Cree**: Indian tribe

"Cree Prophecy"

Only after the last tree has been cut down

Only after the last river has been poisoned

Only after the last fish has been caught

Only then will you find that money cannot be eaten.

TASKS

1 Investigate the irony of the cartoon. What does the goat herder in Mongolia stand for?
2 What message does the cartoon have? Why is it funny? At second thought, is it really funny?
3 What is the message of the "Cree prophecy"? Do you agree?
4 The "Cree prophecy" has occasionally been used as a sticker on cars. Explain the contradiction.

13

"Lessons from Fukushima"

On 11 March 2011, a series of nuclear accidents occurred at the Fukushima Nuclear Power Plant in Japan after it had been struck by a tsunami. What followed was a release of radioactive materials into the air that caused controversial debates about nuclear power around the world. The text below is a press release from February 28, 2012. http://www.greenpeace.org/international/en/press/releases/Lessons-from-Fukushima-nuclear-disaster-report-shows-millions-remain-at-risk.

1 "While triggered by the tragic March 11th earthquake and tsunami, the Fukushima disaster was ultimately caused by the Japanese authorities choosing to ignore risks, and make business a higher priority than safety,"
5 said Jan Vande Putte, Greenpeace International nuclear campaigner. "This report shows that nuclear energy is inherently unsafe, and that governments are quick to approve reactors, but remain ill-equipped to deal with problems and protect people. This has not changed
10 since the Fukushima disaster, and that is why millions of people continue to be exposed to nuclear risks." […]
The report […] reaches three important insights:

1) Japanese authorities and the operators of the Fukushima plant were entirely wrong in their assump-
15 tions about the risks of a serious accident. The real risks were known but downplayed and ignored.

2) Even though Japan is considered one of the best-prepared countries […] for handling major disasters the reality of a large nuclear disaster proved to be far
20 worse than what was planned for. Nuclear emergency and evacuation plans utterly failed to protect people.

3) Hundreds of thousands of people have been deeply affected by evacuations to escape radioactive contami-nation. They cannot rebuild their lives due to a lack of support and financial compensation. Japan is one of 25 only three countries with a law making a nuclear op-erator liable for the full costs of a disaster. Yet, the liability law and compensation schemes are inadequate in Japan. Even a year after the disaster began, impacted people are essentially left on their own and Japanese 30 taxpayers will end up paying much of the costs.

"This disaster was predictable and predicted, but happened because of the age-old story of cutting corners to protect profits over people," said Kazue Suzuki, a Greenpeace Japan Nuclear Campaigner. "The authorities 35 are already recklessly pushing to restart reactors without learning anything from the Fukushima disaster and the people will once again be forced to pay the price of their government's mistakes."

"People should not be forced to live with the myth of 40 nuclear safety and under the shadow of a nuclear disaster waiting to happen," said Vande Putte. "Nuclear power must be phased out and replaced with smart investments in energy efficiency and renewable power. This ap-proach will create millions of sustainable jobs, improve 45 energy independence, reduce greenhouse gas emis-sions, and will also ensure people will never again suffer radioactive fallout from a preventable disaster."

Vocabulary

7 inherently (adv.): a quality that is inherent in s.th. is a natural part of it and cannot be separated from it – **8 approve** (v.): to officially accept a plan, proposal etc – **8 ill-equipped** (adj.): not having the necessary equipment or skills for a particular situation or activity – **11 expose to** (v.): to put s.o. in a situation where they are not protected from s.th. – **14 assumption** (n.): s.th. that you think is true although you have no definite proof – **16 downplay** (v.): to make s.th. seem less important than it really is – **21 utterly** (adv.): completely; used especially to emphasize that s.th. was very bad, or that a feeling was very strong – **27 liable** (adj.): legally responsible for the cost of s.th. – **28 scheme** (n.): an official plan that is intended to help people in some way – **28 inadequate** (adj.): not good enough, big enough, skilled enough etc. for a particular purpose – **29 impact** (v.): to have an important or notice-able effect on s.o. or s.th. – **33 cut corners** (idiom): to save time, money, or energy by doing things quickly and not as carefully as you should – **36 recklessly** (adv.): not caring or worrying about the possible bad or dangerous results of your actions – **43 phase out** (v.): to gradually stop using or providing s.th. – **47 ensure** (v.): to make certain that s.th. will happen properly – **48 fallout** (n.): the dangerous radio-active dust which is left in the air after a nuclear explosion and which slowly falls to earth – **48 preventable** (adj.): capable of being prevented

TASKS

1 What do you know about the Fukushima disaster?
2 List Greenpeace's insights in key words.
3 What makes the text so convincing?
4 Do you share Greenpeace's stance on the dangers of nuclear power plants?
5 Do a research on how Fukushima has changed nuclear policies. Present your findings in class.

14 | The Population Explosion

Some experts have estimated that Earth could carry 40 billion people with the current technology. Others believe that the planet's carrying capacity is infinite. Still others feel that Earth has already exceeded its carrying capacity.

Info

Explosion Expected (compiled from the websites listed below)

A recent United Nations report predicts that by 2050, the world's population will reach about 9.3 billion. While population growth in industrialized countries such as the United States has essentially stopped, growth in less developed countries in Africa, Asia, and Latin America continues to rise. Between the years 1988 and 2000, we added 1 billion people to our world (from 5 to 6 billion), and from 2000 to 2012 another 1 billion (to 7 billion).

Vocabulary/Expression

exceed (v.): /ɪkˈsiːd/ to be more than a particular number or amount – **human carrying capacity**: the maximum number of people Earth can support over the long-term – **population clock** (n.): the threat of overpopulation on Earth

TASK

1 Ask your friends or the members of your class. How many people believe that Earth has already exceeded its carrying capacity? How many believe that Earth's carrying capacity is infinite? Defend your opinion.

INTERNET PROJECT

2 Form groups, each consulting an internet source on the "Population Clock". Then discuss the following factors contributing to changes in population numbers. Suggest solutions.

- Fertility – rate of births.
- Morbidity – the incidence of diseases.
- Mortality – rate of deaths.
- Migration – movement of large groups of people within and across borders.

Start with the entry "World population" in Wikipedia.

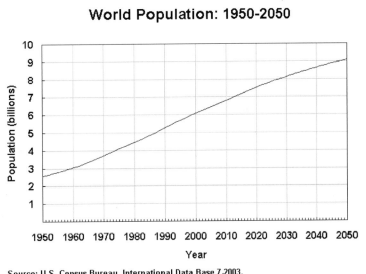

World Population: 1950-2050

Source: U.S. Census Bureau, International Data Base 7-2003.

15 | AIDS: A Global Disease

AIDS (Acquired Immune Deficiency Syndrome) is caused by a virus, HIV (Human Immunodeficiency Virus), first isolated in 1983. It has been identified in over 200 countries and territories worldwide and is spreading rapidly in many affected populations, particularly in developing countries. HIV can only be transmitted directly from person to person, either by sexual contact, exchange of blood or body fluids or from mother to child. HIV incidence and prevalence can vary greatly from country to country and even within countries, depending on several risk factors and risk behaviours. Since the HIV epidemic is driven mainly by sexual transmission, the level and intensity of risk behaviours (unprotected sex) in a given community are the main determinants of the spread of the virus. – In 2011, some 1.7 million people died from AIDS-related causes, a decline of 24% since the peak in 2005. (Sources: www.unaids.org/en/default.asp – www.who.int/en/ – www.aidshilfe.de)

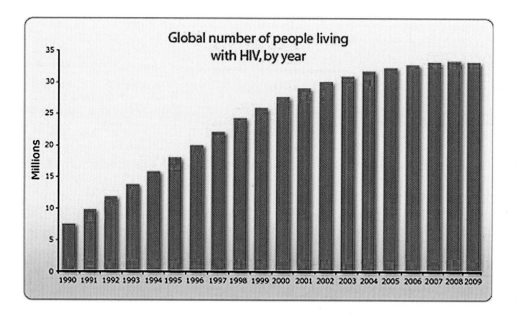

"My Foster Son was Diagnosed with AIDS"

Apart from statistics, the impact of AIDS is possibly best understood or felt if one looks at the lives of individuals – what the virus does to them, their family and friends. The following is a true story, posted on the internet at www.areyouhivprejudiced.org, a website supported by a self-help AIDS organization (15 March 2003).

1 My foster son, Michael, aged 8, was born HIV positive and diagnosed with AIDS at the age of 8 months. While still not expected to survive into adulthood, he is now a lively, bright, active and charming individual. 5 Born to parents who subsequently, and most unexpectedly, discovered that they were both HIV positive, Michael is one of a small but growing number of children in this country who have AIDS. I took on Michael as a foster child three and a half years ago after his 10 mother died of AIDS and his father became too ill to look after him. I took him into our family home, in a small village in the South West [of England]. At first relations with the local school were wonderful and Michael thrived. Only the head teacher and Michael's personal class assistant knew of his illness. 15

Then someone broke confidentiality and told a parent that Michael had AIDS. That parent, of course, told all the others. This caused such panic and hostility that we were forced to move out of the area. Michael was no longer welcome at the school. Other children were not 20 allowed to play with him – instead they jeered and taunted him cruelly. One day a local mother started screaming at us to keep him away from her children and shouting that he should have been put down at birth. Michael heard her. 25

Later Michael said, sadly, "Mummy, why can't I be human like other children?"

Vocabulary

Intro: transmit (v.): to pass from one person to another – **incidence** (n.): the number of times something happens – **prevalence** (n.): being common – **determinant** (n.): something that strongly influences what you do or how you behave – **1 foster son**: adopted son – **5 subsequent** (adj.): following – **14 thrive** (v.): grow and prosper – **14 personal class assistant**: a person at school, a teacher or tutor, who takes special care of this student – **16 confidentiality** (n.): /ˌkɒnfɪˌdenʃɪˈælɪtɪ/ a situation in which you trust someone not to tell secret or private information to anyone else – **18 hostility** (n.): when someone is unfriendly and full of anger towards another person – **21 jeer** (v.): /dʒɪəʳ/ laugh at someone or shout unkind things at them in a way that shows you do not respect them – **22 taunt** (v.): /tɔːnt/ try to make someone angry or upset by saying unkind things to them – **24 put down at birth**: kill at birth

Billboard campaigns to prevent AIDS are launched all over the world. The poster above is from Africa.

AWARENESS

1 What are some of the most common prejudices about AIDS and people with AIDS? Are they true?

2 What do you know about the spread of AIDS?

COMPREHENSION

3 What do the statistics of the chart on p. 36 tell you about the spread of AIDS?

4 Retell the story of Michael from his point of view. Use a first-person narrator.

ANALYSIS

5 What makes Michael's story so moving? Look at the composition of this text.

OPINION

6 How would you react if someone near you told you that he or she was HIV-positive?

7 If this person told you to keep it a secret, would you be able to do so? Be honest to yourself.

INTERNET PROJECT

8 Find out more about AIDS and what you can do to prevent it and to become concerned. Visit www.areyouhivprejudiced.org, a British website.

Global summary of the AIDS epidemic, 2010	
Number of people living with HIV in 2010	
Total	34.0 million [31.6–35.2 million]
Adults	30.1 million [28.4–31.5 million]
Women	16.8 million [15.8–17.6 million]
Children under 15 years	3.4 million [3.0–3.8 million]
People newly infected with HIV in 2010	
Total	2.7 million [2.4–2.9 million]
Adults	2.3 million [2.1–2.5 million]
Children under 15 years	390,000 [340,000–450,000]
AIDS deaths in 2010	
Total	1.8 million [1.6–1.9 million]
Adults	1.5 million [1.4–1.6 million]
Children under 15 years	250,000 [220,000–290,000]

Leslie Lum

"Old Age Gold" (a story about becoming a Canadian citizen)

"Old Age Gold" is a story asking questions about immigration and immigration laws. The author, Leslie Lum, is what might be called a living Chinese-Canadian success story. The busy university teacher, entrepreneur and counsellor of numerous companies is also an author of fiction, having published several stories in prestigious magazines. – Her short story "Old Age Gold" is written mostly from the perspective of an old Chinese lady. Guy Mo Chiang has lived most of her life in a neighbourhood near the Chinatown of Toronto, Canada. She is a simple woman, who has never assimilated to Canadian life and speaks almost no English. She is unhappily married to a husband she calls "old board". To get her "Old Age Gold", that is money to live on now as she is old, she finally has to become a Canadian citizen. She has to attend a citizenship hearing – an official meeting to decide if a person can become a citizen of a country. She is accompanied by two aids, Mrs. Louie and Mrs. Chin. They want to help her get through the hearing, in which a government official asks her a number of questions. Through her eyes, the officer looks like a white bear, and that is what she calls him. – "Old Age Gold," *Introducing New English Literatures.* Ed. Albert-Reiner Glaap (Berlin: Cornelsen, 1994), 57–68. The story has been shortened (see (…)), but not adapted.

1 "What is your name?"

The first question is always the easiest. Mrs. Louie had told her about the Canadian
5 citizenship hearing. In this fluorescent room with wood panel walls, Canadian wood, the first question was easy. There was a kind of order in
10 the government pens and papers. The judge had her file in his hand. She recognized it, her name in print. Name. There was the sound of type-
15 writers behind the wood walls, wood walls with swirls and curls, Canadian wood. Perhaps they were typing her name. The first question was always the easiest after the shock of arrival. They
20 gave chances. They always gave chances, these Canadians. The judge would, this kind-looking man, only forty years or so with his brown glasses. So young a man to have glasses and government papers. He would understand her fright. She thought of the answer. Sur-
25 name last, these funny westerners, surname last as if it did not matter at all, hidden behind the sound of given name. And surname must be given of husband, not father, another complication. How very contrived, a mystery, these westerners and their logic were. She
30 rolled the syllables slowly over on her thin tongue before pronouncing. Everything seemed of the utmost importance as if even the breath must be checked before exhaling. The judge, he might notice some deviation, something that was not Canadian. Guy Mo

Chinatowns can be found all over the world, in London, Manchester, New York, San Francisco, Toronto, Vancouver etc. A Chinatown is an area in a city where there are Chinese restaurants and shops, and where a lot of Chinese people live.

Chiang. Slowly the words came out. It was easy. Merely 35 reverse the name. Guy Mo Chiang.

"When did you come to Canada?"

It was difficult for Guy Mo Chiang to get over here from China. One had to attempt all means in those days, thirty years ago. Actually the fault fell completely 40 on her husband. Completely. He arrived here first. It was he who bought the papers using the assumed name. Such a name too, so far from his own name, especially from hers. There was no other way. They had no relatives who had immigrated. It was necessary 45 to leave China, then. […]

"Do you speak English?"

Of course she would answer yes. Yes, Mrs. Chin told her to say that she was taking night classes at the Catholic school. She wasn't, of course. What possible use could she find for English? Thirty years now, she had not needed it. And now when the return was beginning she finally needed it. The judge was looking at her from behind his huge wood desk filled with papers. He expected an answer. All the women who had passed their citizenship hearing had said yes. Yes, Guy Mo Chiang does speak English. [...] Happy, happy she could speak English. There was no need for it. Everybody in the neighbourhood spoke Chinese. That was why they had never moved out of there. There were many women in the neighbourhood who did not speak English and who had their citizenship papers. Say yes. Mrs. Chin was sitting there nodding at her. Say yes. She spoke enough English to get through this Canadian citizenship hearing. Yes. She did. English, language of the barbarians, for Canadian-borns and westerners. English, not needed in her neighbourhood.

"Where do you live?"

In her neighbourhood the new immigrants always settled first. It was very nice before the government started putting in housing projects. There were only Chinese immigrants. [...] The government gave grants to improve the neighbourhood, to preserve the Chinese culture, probably an apology for having moved in the westerners. [...] This neighbourhood near Chinatown. Guy Mo Chiang could go and argue with the store clerks over which piece of meat they were giving her. She could choose her meat through the glass. They always gave too much fat. She could argue with them. This could change nothing but at least she could speak to them. She went to the supermarket sometimes. It bothered her, all the newness, the shiny freezers, the shelves with everything arranged just so, Western. Many of the stores in Chinatown were like that now but Guy Mo Chiang remained with the older ones, the ones run by the older immigrants and their sons. The supermarkets wrapped their meats already and she could not argue in Chinese.

"Do you work?"

She had worked all her life, all her life. When she first arrived here, there were many jobs, but money, money was scarce. She had worked in a restaurant cleaning dishes. Then like many of the other women she took to farm labour. It was difficult. Up at five o'clock in the morning and into the dark blue truck with Hon Wah Yeung written on the side in white letters. It was only as large as three cars and yet Hon Wah Yeung managed to fit as many as eighty people into the truck, on the hard wooden benches. In the summer, it was young children, teenagers not old enough to get a social insurance number, and the women. Hon Wah Yeung was paid for everybody that he brought onto the farm. He had a young Canadian-born girl punching cards for home during strawberry season. She was very pretty and spoke English. The owner of the farm bought her candy and pinched her cheek. Hon Wah Yeung said be nice to the boss man. He was fogheaded. [...] Ten minutes and it

Pagoda meets skyscraper – East meets West in this picture from San Francisco

would be all over, perhaps six minutes now. She could claim Canadian citizenship. [...] Of course it was better than China; there was running water, food to eat, a room of her own and the rooming house was so close to others. Years ago. Guy Mo Chiang had lost count. It was of no significance, those years of disappointment. She had hoped; she had wished; the relatives had told her that there was nothing but good fortune to be found here. After the first week she had wanted to return. At least in Hong Kong she had worked for a rich family. She was that close to wealth. But then she had lived down those expectations through the years. She became accustomed to hard labour, as in China, as in Hong Kong. But this time there were westerners to tell how hard she was working, working for him. But it would all end now. [...] After seventy years on this earth, life would be finally happy. She would finally have ... a place, a home. Ever since arriving here there had been nothing on her mind but returning to China with Canadian fortune. She, who could neither read nor write the language of China. She, who had spent her life envying her elder sisters who had learned to read a few characters. [...]

"How many children have you?"

Such nice pictures on his desk, this judge had. His children with golden hair and blue eyes. Two of them and so young. That was success, to have such lovely children. They had three children once. One son had died in China. It was too difficult. Their other son was making his fortune in San Francisco. His restaurant was doing much business. Often he wrote, often for such a busy man as he was. He sent money, sometimes. But that old board hoarded it like a cat with a captured bird. Their daughter remained trapped near China with her husband. Guy Mo Chiang would return there and her daughter would take care of her. They sent money to China often and wondered how much went to her and how much the Communists took. She would return with her Canadian Old Age Gold and they would live well. Grandchildren, she would see her grandchildren. Her son sent pictures up at Christmas. He had four children by a Christmas tree. She had wanted four children too, many children, but that old board said there was not enough money. And one had died. They should have had more. They would die. One died easily. More children, more would live. And her son did not have the time to bring her grandchildren up to see her. He had three sons and a daughter and the restaurant where he worked seven days a week. [...] Guy Mo Chiang had never gone to school. She found it difficult to practise these sounds. She did not know how to. Mayors, premiers, prime ministers and commons. [...]

"Who represents the Queen in Canada?"

Guy Mo Chiang was silent for a long time. It was necessary to produce an answer so she could, six weeks from now, stand with fifty other new Canadians and mouth the Oath of Allegiance and take home the Bible and papers to China. The other women had told her about the ceremony. How one stood and repeated the sounds. There were speeches and tea after. It was necessary to find an answer. It was difficult. There were so many obstacles, lack of place, lack of time, lack of money, lack of success. But success was only a few minutes away. He looked a kind man, the white bear. Perhaps he would overlook this one wrong answer, just one wrong answer. The sounds were becoming unfamiliar.

"Who represents the Queen?"

Queen. He emphasized the sound "queen". It was of some importance. The prime minister was an important sound. Was he not the centre of everything, like an emperor? They said China was different now. The new immigrants came back with stories of improvement of conditions, revolution. The prime minister was connected to it somehow. [...]

"Where does the Queen live?"

Guy Mo Chiang stopped smiling. Mrs. Louie and Mrs. Chin sat upright in their chairs, silently mouthing words to her. The white bear was looking at her. There was silence and the only breathing was the white bear. He was looking at her in his brown suit and brown glasses. He was looking at Guy Mo Chiang as if she did not belong in Canada. He was stopping her from returning to where she did belong.

"Where does the Queen live?"

The white bear was speaking again. It was different in China, the Communists. Guy Mo Chiang was thinking of her daughter and her two grandchildren. She thought of her son who was too busy to visit her. It was too difficult to go down to visit him and her grandchildren. San Francisco was so far away and besides the old board would not come with her. She would have to travel alone. Back to China. Alone. The old board, he would be alone. Her daughter was not eating well. Perhaps the Communists would take away her Old Age Gold cheque. It was different now. The new immigrants laughed at the old ones. They said they had kept the customs of old China. There was no such China now.

The white bear was shuffling the papers again. He looked up at Guy Mo Chiang. She looked as if she might cry. The poor old stooped lady. "She's old. It is difficult for her to learn, but she has worked so hard."

Mrs. Chin was speaking loudly to him.

"I can see that. I can see that." The white bear was speaking.

"It is her greatest wish to become a Canadian, to belong to Canada."

Mrs. Chin folded her hands together and pleaded with the judge.

The judge looked at Guy Mo Chiang. Canada was a place for all. Equal opportunity for all races, cultures and ages. It was the glossy slick book they handed out to all their applicants for citizenship. She was so old and stooped. She looked as if she had no place in the world.

235 "I spoke English once like that." Mrs. Louie nodded at the judge. "I learned better now. See. She was learning. She is very clever. She babysits. She will pick it up from the children. When she stays a while longer in Canada she will learn very well."

240 The white bear looked at them. He looked at Guy Mo Chiang. Guy Mo Chiang watched China disappear. It was better this way. She could argue with the store clerks. China, after thirty years, why had she ever thought of it. She could never belong.

245 The white bear was speaking.

"Mrs. Chiang, I want you to come back in about a month for your citizenship papers. We'll notify you when to come."

He looked at Mrs. Chin. Guy Mo Chiang looked at 250 Mrs. Chin. "Can you explain to her and tell her to bring pictures?"

Mrs. Chin nodded and smiled. She told Guy Mo Chiang that she must bring pictures so that she could have a card made up showing her Canadian citizenship. Canadian citizenship. Mrs. Louie was smiling at the 255 judge. Guy Mo Chiang looked at them all.

The white bear was speaking again.

"She has done very well … very well. We give the older ones more chances. The names are hard to learn."

The white bear smiled. He pushed up his glasses. 260 Such a nice man.

The red and white flag behind, the printing on the wall in black frames, they all said something about Canada. They were all smiling. Perhaps Guy Mo Chiang would go down to visit her son in San Francisco now 265 that she had her Canadian citizenship and Old Age Gold. China was so far away.

Vocabulary

6 fluorescent (adj.): having a very harsh, bright light – **16 swirls and curls** (n.): circular and curved patterns – **24 fright** (n.): fear – **26 given name**: first name – **28 contrived** (adj.): /kən'traɪvd/ unnatural, artificial – **33 exhale** (v.): /eks'heɪl/ breathe out – **34 deviation** (n.): /ˌdiːvɪ'eɪʃən/ behaviour which is not acceptable or normal – **36 reverse** (v.): change the order by putting the first thing last – **72 grant** (n.): money given for a particular purpose – **113 punch cards**: fill out forms indicating how long sb. has worked in a day – **117 pinch** (v.): squeeze between thumb and first finger – **119 fog-headed** (coll.): not very clever – **153 old board** (coll.): (here) old man – **153 hoard** (v.): accumulate s.th. and hide it away – **220 stooped** (adj.): /stuːpd/ having the back and shoulders rounded – **227 plead with** (v.): /pliːd/ (here) to beg – **232 applicant** (n.): someone who has formally asked for s.th. – **243 clerk** (n.): someone who keeps records or accounts in an office

Explanation

177 Oath of Allegiance: [əʊθ əv ə'liːdʒəns] a speech which is a promise to respect Canada and be loyal to it. In the USA this is called the Pledge of Allegiance (spoken every morning at school, while looking at the national flag and putting one's right hand over one's heart).

AWARENESS

1 Should immigrants have some basic knowledge of their new country? Should they be able to speak its language? Why? Discuss with others.
2 Why do people want to emigrate to a different country like the USA, Canada or Australia? Have you ever thought that emigration could be a choice for you? Why / Why not?

COMPREHENSION

3 Describe exactly what you learn about the setting, the characters and the events in the short story. Can you make a short sketch of the office? What does it reveal?
4 What do you learn about Guy Mo Chiang's life? Write down the main facts of her life, beginning from her birth in China up to this hearing.
5 Is she able to answer the official's questions? Look closely at the text.
6 Describe the official's reaction. Do you think that this is the typical reaction of a government official?
7 How does the old lady react in the end?

ANALYSIS

8 Why is this short story comparatively easy to read? Does this make the story less artful?

9 Compare the difference between the time which is narrated in the story and the narrating time. What does it reveal about the story's structure?

10 What is the perspective used in most parts of the story? Look at a number of passages and analyse whether the reader gets different points of view. How does this influence you as a reader?

11 Characterise the old lady. Pay attention to the fact that she characterises herself through her thoughts.

12 Describe how her life and her way of thinking are different (from the average Canadian's, from yours, etc.).

13 Why has she made no effort to assimilate to Canada? Give reasons with reference to her thoughts.

OPINION

14 Do you think the old lady deserves her "Old Age Gold"?

15 What do you think made the official accept her as a Canadian citizen?

16 Are there similar people like the old lady in your country? What do you know about them? Should the government support them?

17 Do you think that the lady's life and opinions are typical of poorer immigrants?

18 After all, does the story have a message?

PROJECTS

19 Consider asylum seekers and 'guest workers' (immigrant workers) whom you know about in your country. Why do they want to stay? Do they plan on going back? Will they go back in the end?

20 Compare the situation of Chinese-Canadians with that of immigrants in your country. How much immigration is permitted into Canada and your country now, and from what countries? How are potential immigrants and visitors from other countries treated in these countries? For Canada, visit http://www.cic.gc.ca/.

21 Find out about Chinese communities in other parts of the world (e.g. in the U.K., U.S.A., Singapore, Australia). Also, find out more about Chinatowns worldwide. Visit http://www.chinatown-online.co.uk/ or the website for Chinatown Toronto: http://www.landiss.com/chinatown01.htm.

Postcolonial literature

The English language belongs not only to the British and Americans, but also to millions of other people throughout the five continents. The last decades have seen the emergence of the exciting New Literatures in English (or 'postcolonial literature') from the countries of the former British Empire. They express the experience of people from all over the world struggling to achieve economic independence and find their own cultural voice and identity. If you are looking for a selection of novels, short stories, dramas and poems from this field, read the volume *The Postcolonial Experience: Decolonizing the Mind* from the Viewfinder series. To gain further insights into 'postcolonial' mentalities, read short stories from the following compilations: *Introducing New English Literatures*. Ed. Albert-Reiner Glaap. Berlin: Cornelsen (see also p. 38), 1994; *Many Voices – Many Cultures. Multicultural British Short Stories*. Ed. Barbara Korte, Claudia Sternberg. Stuttgart: Reclam, 1997; a number of short stories from the collection *Tales from the Global Village* (München: Langenscheidt, 2006) also have a postcolonial context.

17 | Bill Gates

The Road Ahead

William "Bill" Gates (born 1955) is chairman and chief software architect of Microsoft Corporation, one of the world's leading companies. He is not only one of the richest people in the world, but also a living example of the American success story. His unbounded optimism and belief in the personal computer, the internet and information technology (=IT) in general are expressed in his bestselling book *The Road Ahead*. In it he develops his vision of a world in which everybody is interconnected globally by interactive computer networks. For Bill Gates, the spread of the Information Age will transform all our lives for the better. In the following excerpt from the book he writes about the need to adapt to the Information Age – and its benefits. – Bill Gates, *The Road Ahead: Completely Revised and Updated* (Harmondsworth: Penguin, 1996), 294, 298.

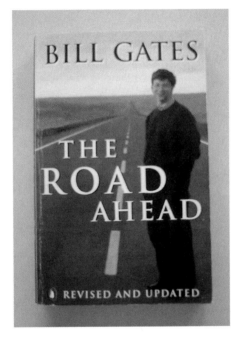

1 The younger you are, the more important it is that you adapt. If you're fifty or older today, you may be out of the workforce be-
5 fore you'll need to use a computer – although I think that if you don't learn you'll be missing out on the chance for some meaningful experiences. But if you're
10 twenty-five today and not comfortable with computers, you risk being ineffective in almost any kind of work you pursue.

Ultimately, the interactive net-
15 work isn't for my generation or the one before me. It's for future generations. The kids who have grown up with PCs in the last decade, and the kids who will
20 grow up with the network in the next, will push the technology to its limits.

We have to pay particular attention to correcting the gender imbalance. When I was young, it seemed that only boys were encouraged to mess around with
25 computers. Girls are far more active with computers today than they were two decades ago, but there are still many fewer women than men in technical careers. By making sure that girls as well as boys get comfortable with computers at an early age, we can ensure that
30 both sexes enjoy their rightful share of the good jobs that are available to people with computer expertise.

My own experience as a child and the experience of my friends raising children today is that, once a child is exposed to computing, he or she is hooked. But we
35 have to create the opportunity for that exposure. Schools should have low-cost access to computers connected to the interactive network, and teachers need to become comfortable with the new tools. One of the wonderful things about the interactive network
40 is that virtual equity can be achieved much more easily than real-world equity. It would take a massive amount of money to give every grammar school in every poor area the same library resources as the good schools in Beverly Hills.
45 But when you put schools online, they all get the same access to information, wherever it might be stored. We are all created equal in the virtual world, and
50 we can use this equality to help address some of the sociological problems that society has yet to solve in the physical world. The network won't eliminate barriers
55 of inequality and prejudice, but it will be a powerful force in that direction. […]

The presence of advanced communications systems prom-
60 ises to make countries more alike and reduce the importance of national boundaries. The fax machine, the portable video camera, and Cable News Network are among the forces that brought about the end of communist regimes and the Cold War be-
65 cause they enabled news to pass both ways through the Iron Curtain. […]

The new access to information can draw people together by increasing their understanding of other cultures. But commercial satellite broadcasts to coun-
70 tries such as China and Iran offer citizens glimpses of the outside world that are not necessarily sanctioned by their governments. Some governments are afraid that such exposure will cause discontent and worse, a "revolution of expectations" when disenfranchised people get
75 enough information about another lifestyle to contrast it with their own. Within individual societies, the balance between traditional and modern experiences is bound to shift as people use the network to expose themselves to a greater range of possibilities. Some cultures may feel
80 under assault as people pay greater attention to global issues and cultures and less to their traditional local ones.

Vocabulary

13 pursue (v.): /pə'sjuː/ wish to have - **23 gender imbalance** (n.): uneven chances and different interests depending on whether you are male or female - **24 mess around with**: toy with - **31 expertise** (n.): /ˌekspə'tiːz/ special skills or knowledge in a particular subject - **34 expose to** (v.): show something that is usually covered or hidden - **34 hooked** (adj.): caught, addicted - **40 equity** (n.): /'ekwɪti/ a situation in which all people are treated equally and no one has an unfair advantage - **55 eliminate** (v.): /ɪ'lɪmɪneɪt/ to completely get rid of something - **70 broadcast** (v.): to send out radio or television programmes - **71 glimpse** (n.): a look at - **72 sanction** (v.): to officially accept or allow something - **74 exposure** (n.): experience of new things - **74 discontent** (n.): a feeling of being unhappy and not satisfied with the situation you are in - **75 disenfranchised** (adj.): /ˌdɪsɪn'fræntʃaɪzd/ not having any rights, especially the right to vote, and not feeling part of society - **78 is bound to**: will certainly - **81 assault** (n.): attack

Explanations

14 interactive network: computer systems or computer games which allow you to communicate directly with them - **63 Cable News Network**: a US news network on television, paid for by the person watching it - **65 Cold War**: the unfriendly relationship between the US and the Soviet Union after the Second World War - **67 Iron Curtain**: the name that was used for the border between the Communist countries of Eastern Europe and the rest of Europe

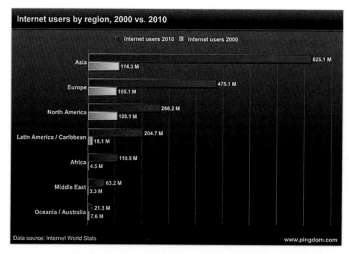

Internet users by region, 2000 vs. 2010

AWARENESS

1 How is your life formed by the tools of the Information Age? Could you "survive" without your mobile phone, your PC, the internet, e-mail access, etc.?

COMPREHENSION

2 Make a list of all the technical terms used in the article. Do you understand them all? If not, does that make you "IT-illiterate" and therefore unfit for the Information Age?
3 What, according to Gates, are the IT challenges for the young generation? Can you meet them?
4 Make a list of all the advantages of IT – past and future – Gates enumerates in this text.
5 What are the reasons Gates gives for his optimism?

ANALYSIS

6 Provide a summary of Gates' line of argument.
7 "The younger you are, the more important it is that you adapt" (l. 1f.). Adapt to what and why? Base your answer on quotations from the text.
8 What does the term "gender imbalance" (l. 23) express?
9 Explain the term "virtual equity" (l. 40).
10 Why and how would private corporations finance school networks? Consider the problems of such ventures.

OPINION

11 How is worldwide equality via information technology achieved? Discuss Gates' vision and develop counter-arguments. Use information from the chart above.
12 Do you agree that the fax machine contributed to the end of Communism? Or that new technologies in general brought about the fall of the Wall? Is this an exaggeration?
13 Does easier exchange of information lead to less intercultural misunderstanding, as suggested by Gates? Think about examples from your own life.

18 David Lodge

"Tourism Is Wearing Out the Planet"

Born in 1935 and educated at University College London, David Lodge is one of the best-known authors of campus or university novels such as *Changing Places* (1975), *Small World* (1984) and *Nice Work* (1988). While these fictions display his gift for satirical and ironic descriptions of life in an academic environment, *Paradise News* (1991) revolves around the issue of travelling, specifically mass tourism, as experienced on the beautiful island of Hawaii. The island seems to be flooded with tourists, the novel's protagonist Bernard Walsh being one of them. This is put into a global perspective by one of the other characters of the novel, Roger Sheldrake, an academic doing research in tourism. He reflects on tourism as a new quasi-religion in the following excerpt. – David Lodge, *Paradise News* (Harmondsworth: Penguin, 1992), 78–79.

1 "Tourism is wearing out the planet." Sheldrake delved into his silvery attaché case again and brought out a sheaf of press-cuttings marked with yellow highlighter. He flipped through them. "The footpaths in the Lake
5 District have become trenches. The frescos in the Sistine Chapel are being damaged by the breath and body-heat of spectators. A hundred and eight people enter Notre Dame every minute: their feet are eroding the floor and the buses that bring them there are rotting the stone-
10 work with exhaust fumes. Pollution from cars queueing to get to Alpine ski resorts is killing the trees and caus-ing avalanches and landslides. The Mediterranean is like a toilet without a chain: you have a one in six chance of getting an infection if you swim in it. In
15 1987 they had to close Venice one day because it was full. In 1963 forty-four people went down the Colorado river on a raft, now there are a thousand trips a day. In 1939 a million people travelled abroad; last year it was four hundred million. By the year 2000 there could be six hundred and fifty million international travellers, 20 and five times as many people travelling in their own countries. The mere consumption of energy entailed is stupendous."

"My goodness," said Bernard.

"The only way to put a stop to it, short of legislation, is 25 to demonstrate to people that they aren't really enjoying themselves when they go on holiday, but engaging in a superstitious ritual. It's no coincidence that tourism arose just as religion went into decline. It's the new opium of the people, and must be exposed as such." 30

"Won't you do yourself out of a job, if you're success-ful?" said Bernard.

"I don't think there's any immediate risk of that," said Sheldrake, surveying the crowded lounge.

The Lake District – one of the most idyllic places in England, but also a major tourist destination

Vocabulary

1 wear out (v.): to damage, ruin, exhaust - **1 delve** (v.): to search by putting your hand deeply into it - **2 attaché case** (n.): a thin case used for carrying business documents - **3 sheaf** (n.): several pieces of paper held or tied together - **3 press-cutting** (n.): a short piece of writing or a picture, cut out from a newspaper or magazine - **5 trench** (n.): a long narrow hole dug into the surface of the ground - **5 fresco** (n.): a painting made on a wall while the plaster is still wet - **8 erode** (v.): gradually destroying the surface - **10 exhaust fumes** (n.): /ɪɡ'zɔːst/ waste gasses from cars - **12 avalanche** (n.): /'ævəlɑːnʃ/ a large mass of snow, ice, and rocks that falls down the side of a mountain (similar to landslide) - **17 raft** (n.): /rɑːft/ a flat floating structure, usually made of pieces of wood tied together, used as a boat - **22 consumption** (n.): the act of buying and using products - **22 entail** (v.): /ɪn'teɪl/ to involve something as a necessary part or result - **23**

stupendous (adj.): surprisingly large or impressive - **28 superstitious** (adj.): /ˌsuːpə'stɪʃəs/ strongly influenced by a belief which is not based on fact or reason but on old ideas about luck, magic, etc. - **28 coincidence** (n.): sth. which happens by chance

Explanations

4 Lake District: an area in northwest England famous for its beautiful lakes and mountains and visited by many tourists - **5 Sistine Chapel**: a chapel in the Vatican, Rome, famous for the paintings on its ceiling done by Michaelangelo - **7 Notre Dame**: a famous cathedral in central Paris, which is a beautiful Gothic building from the 12th century

AWARENESS

1 "Tourism is wearing out the planet." Think about the impact of world-wide tourism on your country or area. Then consider how your behaviour as a tourist has contributed to changes in the places you have visited.

2 Robert Runcie observed in 1988: "In the Middle Ages people were tourists because of their religion, whereas now they are tourists because tourism is their religion." Comment on this aphorism.

COMPREHENSION

3 In sum, what negative effects do the examples mentioned in the text have on the environment?

4 Can you add examples from your own experience or knowledge?

ANALYSIS

5 What is Sheldrake driving at? What is his overall message?

6 What effect does Sheldrake's argument have on the reader?

7 How does he achieve this effect? Comment on the style and rhetoric of his little speech.

OPINION

8 Should there be restrictions to travelling?

9 Could you think of possible solutions like imposing quotas, demanding "minimal-knowledge/awareness-tests" in "sensitive areas"? Exchange your opinion with others.

PROJECTS

10 Compare past, present and future destination countries for travelling and holidays. Use the internet as your source.

11 Discuss possible developments and impacts on people and the environment.

Suggested Further Reading

Find out more about David Lodge's immensely readable novels. If you are interested in campus fiction, why not read some of the 'classics' and much emulated stories by the former professor of English literature: the satirical campus-novel about an exchange between Great Britain and the USA, *Changing Places*, or *Small World*, a romantic tale set in the jet-set world of international conferences; *Nice Work* deals with the love affair between a lecturer in English and a company director.

19 William Sutcliffe

Are You Experienced?

William Sutcliffe was born in 1971. The Londoner is the author of several bestsellers, *New Boy*, *The Love Hexagon*, *Whatever Makes You Happy* and *Are You Experienced?*. His novels have been hugely successful and have been translated into twenty languages. The adventures and misadventures of 19-year-old Dave, a cynical young man who uses his 'gap year' between school and university for a big exotic journey through India, are related in *Are You Experienced?*, which was first published in 1997. A hilarious, enormously readable satire on backpackers who are only interested in 'getting to know themselves' and mostly ignorant of India and its people, the novel narrates Dave's experiences as a rite of passage into adulthood – he returns a wiser, more 'experienced' man. Below you find two passages from the novel. The first one takes place in a train station in the middle of India, with Dave and a journalist from Great Britain as the only foreigners. Here the first-person narrator Dave gets a severe dressing-down. The journalist accuses him – and with him his generation – of being completely uninterested in India and the Third World. In the second passage, David takes the Bus to Goa, formerly a hippie 'hang-out', today a place of mass-tourism.
– William Sutcliffe, *Are You Experienced?* (Harmondsworth: Penguin, 1997), 139f., 142f.

1 'I might do an article on you,' he said. [...] 'About me? What have you got to say about me?' 'I'm not sure. Tell me – what do you do all day?' 'What do I do?' [...] I gave him a suspicious look. 'You know – I'm travelling.
5 I'm a backpacker.' 'But what do you do all day? How come you don't get bored?' 'Bored? You could never get bored here.' 'What do you *do*, though? In each place.' He looked genuinely interested. 'Well, you get there. Look for a hotel. Hang out there for a bit. Look
10 around town for a few days. Eat. Read. Sleep. Talk to other travellers. Think about where to go next, then – you know – it's a big hassle to get the tickets for your next journey, so you prepare yourself for that. Then bite the bullet, spend a morning queuing for tickets,
15 and the next day you move on.' 'Right. So the most significant and challenging thing you do in each place is to buy the tickets for getting to the next place.' 'No. I didn't say that.' 'Yes you did.' [...] 'It's fine. I've got more than enough material already.' 'Like what? What
20 are you going to write about me then?' 'I think … something about how it's not hippies on a spiritual mission who come here any more, just morons on a poverty-tourism adventure holiday. The real point would have to be about how going to India isn't an act
25 of rebellion these days, it's actually a form of conformity for ambitious middle-class kids who want to be able to put something on their CV that shows a bit of initiative. All the top companies want robots with initiative these days, and coming to the Third World is the ideal hoop
30 for you to leap through. You come here and cling to each other as if you're on some kind of extended management-bonding exercise in Epping Forest. Then,

having got the nasty business of travel out of the way, you can go home and prove to employers that you are more than ready to settle down for a life of drudgery. I 35 suppose you could call it a modern form of ritual circumcision – it's a badge of suffering you have to wear to be welcomed into the tribe of Britain's future élite. Your kind of travel is all about low horizons dressed up as open-mindedness. You have no interest 40 in India and no sensitivity for the problems this country is trying to face up to. You also treat Indians with a mixture of contempt and suspicion which is reminiscent of the Victorian colonials. Your presence here, in my opinion, is offensive. The whole lot of you should fuck 45 off back to Surrey.'

[...]

In Bombay, I only needed to take one sniff of the city to realize that I couldn't face staying, and walked to the nearest travel agent to buy a ticket for the first bus to 50 Goa (quicker than the train at mere sixteen hours, according to The Book). The bus was due to leave in two hours, actually left in four hours, and took three more hours to reach the edge of Bombay. Once we reached the open road, it was already after midnight, 55 so I decided to try and fall asleep just as the driver put a tape of Hindi musicals on at top volume. This tape played all night, periodically interrupted by me standing up and shouting at him to turn it down. When I did this, everyone on the bus stared at me as if I was mad. 60 Apparently, it was common practice for bus drivers to play music to help keep themselves awake while they drove through the night. At one of our innumerable stops, I bought a box of biscuits from a road-side stall

65 so that I could tear off strips of cardboard in order to improvize a set of ear-plugs, which, it turned out, didn't make any difference to the noise, kept on falling out, and gave me sore ears. I also ate all the biscuits in one go, just to try and take my mind off things, which made 70 me feel sick. The bus broke down half-way through the following day, and I ended up hitchhiking to Panjim (the capital of Goa) in the back of a truck, with a pile of axles for my seat. In a delirium of anger, frustration, loneliness and arse pain, I just about managed to face the one final leg of journey, which was to take a local 75 bus out of the city to the beach. I didn't care where it was going, or which resort I ended up in as long as there was a beach. I had clearly been wrong about the joys of travelling.

Vocabulary

4 suspicious (adj.): thinking that someone might be guilty of doing something wrong or dishonest – **8 genuine** (adj.): sincere, real – **13 hassle** (n.): /'hæsl/ something that is annoying, because it causes problems or is difficult to do – **13 bite the bullet** (v.): do something unpleasant – **21 spiritual mission** (n.): religious work that involves going to a foreign country in order to teach people about Christianity or help poor people – **22 moron** (n.): idiot – **25 conformity** (n.): behaviour that obeys the accepted rules of society or a group – **26 ambitious** (adj.): determined to be successful, rich, powerful etc. – **27 CV**: curriculum vitae, a short written document that lists your education and previous jobs, which you send to employers when you are looking for a job – **29 leap through a hoop** (n.): usually performed in a circus by animals: jump through something resembling a circle – **31 extended management-bonding exercise** (n.): a course for bosses to create more team spirit – **35 drudgery** (n.): hard, boring work – **37 circumcision** (n.): surgical removal of the foreskin of the penis; here referring to a ritual – **37 badge of suffering** (n.): a sign, e.g. a medal that one has suffered and been brave, usually in war – **38 tribe** (n.): usually: a social group consisting of people of the same race – **41 sensitivity** (n.): the ability to understand other people's feelings and problems – **43 contempt** (n.): a feeling that someone or something is not important and deserves no respect – **43 reminiscent of** (adj.): reminding of – **45 offensive** (adj.): very rude or insulting and likely to upset people – **48 sniff** (n.): informal: a small amount or sign of – **58 periodically** (adv.): a number of times, usually at regular times – **64 stall** (n.): a small shop with an open front – **66 ear-plugs** (n.): something you put into your ears so as not to hear what is happening around you – **68 sore** (adj.): painful – **69 take my mind off things**: so I would not worry – **73 axle** (n.): /'æksl/ the bar connecting two wheels on a car or other vehicle – **74 arse** (n.): (vulgar) the part of your body that you sit on – **75 leg** (n.): (here) part – **77 resort** (n.): a place where a lot of people go for holidays

Explanations

32 Epping Forest: a forest in Great Britain – **44 Victorian colonials**: the officials who would run the British Empire in the age of Queen Victoria (1837–1901) – **46 Surrey**: a county in southeast England which is one of the Home Counties. Many of the people who live there travel to London every day to work, and most people think of Surrey as a wealthy, mainly middle-class area – **52 The Book**: allusion to one of the main tourist guides for students and backpackers, *Lonely Planet* (see page 49) – **57 Hindi**: an official language in India

AWARENESS

1 What is the difference between mass tourism and alternative tourism?
2 In the long run, will hardened backpackers pave the way for club med tourists?

COMPREHENSION

3 Make sure you understand who is speaking in each case, David or the journalist.
4 Describe David's daily routine as a tourist in India.
5 Why does the journalist object to this sort of tourism?
6 Why does he tell David that he should go back to Britain?
7 Retell the events of part 2 in your own words.
8 Why is travelling so hard for Dave?

ANALYSIS

9 Take a closer look at Dave's description of his everyday life in India. How does he himself reveal that he is not really interested in India?
10 Make a list of all the accusations the journalists holds against Dave.
11 What does the term "hippies on a spiritual mission" (line 21) imply?
12 What is meant by the expression "poverty-tourism adventure holiday" (line 23)?
13 What exactly is the journalist driving at with the expression that the "Third World is the ideal hoop for you to leap through" (line 29)?
14 Describe the overall impact of the journalist's speech. How does he achieve this impact?
15 How are humour and satire created in part two of the text?
16 What is implied by Dave's remark about "the joys of travelling" (line 79)?

OPINION

17 Do you agree with the journalist and his opinion of Dave?

18 Do you feel that this critique would also apply to your way of travelling?

19 What would be alternative ways of travelling?

20 Comment on Dave's reaction to the Hindi musicals being played on the coach.

21 What are the problems you could encounter when following travel guides like *Lonely Planet*?

PROJECTS

22 **Ecotourism:** Find out about alternative forms of tourism, often called "soft tourism", "responsible tourism", "green tourism", "nature tourism". Ecotourism is about ways of how local populations are able to direct tourism activities and benefit from them. A fair share of the profits goes back to the local community; it contributes to the conservation of biodiversity and shows respect to traditional cultures and social structures. Visit the following websites and write a short report:
www.planeta.com/ecotravel/resources/rtp/globalization.html
www.eduweb.com/schaller/Section2RioBlanco.html
www.andeantravelweb.com/peru/ecotourism (for a specific example)

23 **More about backpackers and shoestring travellers:** Listen to the song "Down Under" by the Australian rock group *Men at Work*. Apart from being a hymn of the backpacker generation, it serves as a semi-official national anthem of the country "down under", Australia. In it, the funny tales of Australian globetrotters are told. Find out about the many allusions in the song.

24 **Tourist guides:** Visit the websites of some of the most-coveted tourist guides. Find out about their presentations of different countries. What sort of tourism do they promote? How do they inform tourists about your country? Do you agree? (Small Planet, Lonely Planet, Let's Go, Baedeker, James Cook, Apa Guides, Marco Polo)

25 **Tourism boards:** Visit the tourism board of a number of countries and describe how the countries present themselves.

Lonely planet
India
The bestselling guide to the subcontinent

Suggested Further Reading

Read *Are You Experienced?* by William Sutcliffe. It is an extremely funny book, full of insights into the psyche of young travellers. As one reviewer remarks: "Witty dialogues, colourful characters and very realistic painful situations make this a great satire on the backpack generation."

Info

Vocabulary: "Travel"

Comment on the following phrases, sayings and quotations:

Phrases:
– as the crow flies: in a straight line
– the back of beyond: a very remote place
– the ends of the earth: the most distant regions of the earth
– the middle of nowhere: a remote and inaccessible place
– off the beaten track: away from the well-frequented route, out of well-known territory
– to boldly go: explore freely (from *Starship Enterprise*)
– wild blue yonder: the far distance; a remote place
– the world's end: the farthest limit of the earth; the farthest attainable point of travel
– to travel on a shoestring: to travel on a low budget
– the world is your oyster: you are at home everywhere

Sayings:
– Go abroad and you'll hear news of home.
– Travel broadens the mind.

Quotations:
– Travelling is the ruin of all happiness! / There's no looking at a building here after seeing Italy. (Fanny Burney, 1752–1840, *Cecilia*, 1782)
– Go West, young man, go West! (John L.B. Soule, 1815–91, *Terre Haute Express*, 1851)
– For my part, I travel not to go anywhere, but to go. I travel for travel's sake. The great affair is to move. (Robert Louis Stevenson, 1850–94, *Virginibus Puerisque*, 1881)
– A man travels the world in search of what he needs and returns home to find it. (George Moore, 1852–1933, *The Brook Kerith*, 1916)

20 "The Nowhere Man"

Pico Iyer

Born in England to Indian parents, Pico Iyer was educated at Eton, Oxford and Harvard. Currently dividing his life between California and Japan, Iyer is a renowned regular contributor to international magazines and a writer of non-fiction. His articles explore how our world is shaped by the way cultures interact, collide and coexist. Drawing on his personal experiences, he relates in his writings extraordinary insights into the way the global and the local meet. – Pico Iyer, "The Nowhere Man", *Observer*, February 16, 1997.

1 By the time I was nine, I was already used to going to school by transatlantic plane, to sleeping in airports, to shuttling back and forth three times a year, between my parents' Indian home in California and my boarding
5 school in England. While I was growing up, I was never within 6,000 miles of the nearest relative. From the time I was a teenager, I took it for granted that I could take my budget vacations in Bolivia and Tibet, China and Morocco. It never seemed strange to me that a girl-
10 friend might be ten hours flying time away, that my closest friends might be on the other side of a continent.

It was only recently that I realised that all these habits of mind and life would scarcely have been imaginable in my parents' youth; that the very facts and facilities
15 that shape my world are all distinctly new developments, and mark me as a modern type. It was only recently, in fact, that I realised that I am an example, perhaps, of an entirely new breed of people, a transcontinental tribe of wanderers that is multiplying as fast as international
20 telephone lines and frequent flyer programmes. We are the transit loungers, forever heading to the departure gate. We buy our interests duty-free, we eat our food on plastic plates, we watch the world through borrowed headphones. We pass through countries as through
25 revolving doors, impermanent residents of nowhere. Nothing is strange to us, and nowhere is foreign. We are visitors even in our own homes. […]

This kind of life offers an unprecedented sense of freedom and mobility: tied down nowhere, we can pick
30 and choose among locations. Ours is the first generation that can go off to visit Tibet for a week, or meet Tibetans down the street. At a superficial level, this new internationalism means that I can meet, in the Hilton coffee shop, an Indonesian businessman who is
35 as conversant as I am with Magic Johnson and Madonna. At a deeper level, it means that I need never feel estranged. If all the world is alien to us, all the world is home.

I have learned to love foreignness. In any place I
40 visit, I have the privileges of an outsider: I am an object of interest, and even fascination; I am a person set apart, able to enjoy the benefits of the place without paying

the taxes. And the places themselves seem glamourous to me – romantic – as seen through foreign eyes: distance on both sides lends enchantment. Policemen let 45 me off speeding tickets, girls want to hear the story of my life, pedestrians will gladly point me to the nearest golden arches. Perpetual foreigners in the transit lounge, we enjoy a kind of diplomatic immunity; and, living off room service in our hotel rooms, we are never 50 obliged to grow up, or even, really, to be ourselves.

And yet, sometimes, I stop myself and think. What kind of heart is being produced by these new changes? Must I always be a None of the Above? When the stewardess presents me with disembarkation forms, 55 what do I fill in? My passport says one thing, my face another. My accent contradicts my eyes. Place of residence, final destination, even marital status are not much easier to fill in; usually, I just tick "other".

Beneath all the boxes, where do we place ourselves? 60 How does one fix a moving object on a map? I am not an exile, really, nor an immigrant; not deracinated, I think, any more than I am rooted. I have not felt the oppression of war, nor found ostracism in the places where I do alight; I scarcely feel severed from a home 65 I have scarcely known. Yet is "citizen of the world" enough to comfort me?

Alienation, we are taught from kindergarten onwards, is the condition of our time. This is the century of exiles and refugees, of boat people and statelessness; 70 the time when traditions have been abolished, and men become closer to machines. This is the century of estrangement: one third of all Afghans live outside of Afghanistan; the second city of the Khmers is a refugee camp; the second tongue of Beverly Hills is Farsi. […] 75

We airport hoppers can, in fact, go through the world as through a house of wonders, picking up something at every stop, and taking the whole globe as our playpen. And we can mix and match as the situation demands. "Nobody's history is my history," Kazuo Ishiguro, a 80 great spokesman for the privileged homeless, once said to me, and went on, "Whenever it was convenient for me to become very Japanese, I could become very Japanese, and then, when I wanted to drop it, I would just become this ordinary Englishman." Instantly, I felt a shock of recognition: I have a wardrobe of selves from which to choose, and I savour the luxury of being able to be an Indian in Cuba (where people are starving for Yoga and Rabindranath Tagore), an American in Thailand or an Englishman in New York. […]

Unable to get stirred by the raising of a flag, we are sometimes unable to see how *anyone* could be stirred. I sometimes think that this is how Salman Rushdie, the great analyst of this condition, somehow became its victim. He had juggled homes for so long, that he forgot how the world looks to someone who is rooted – in country or belief. He had chosen to live so far from affiliation that he could no longer see why people choose affiliation in the first place. Besides, being part of no society means one is accountable to no one, and need respect no laws outside one's own. If single nation people can be fanatical as terrorists, we can end up ineffectual as peace keepers.

We become, in fact, strangers to belief itself, unable to comprehend many of the rages and dogmas that animate (and unite) people. Conflict itself seems inexplicable to us, because partisanship is; we have the agnostic's inability to retrace the steps of faith. I could not begin to fathom why some Muslims would think of murder after hearing about *The Satanic Verses*: yet sometimes I force myself to recall that it is we, in our floating scepticism, who are the exceptions, that in China or Iran, Korea or Peru, it is not so strange to give up one's life for a cause.

We end up, then, a little like non-aligned nations, comfirming our reservations at every step. We tell ourselves, self-servingly, that nationalism breeds monsters, and choose to ignore the fact that internationalism breeds them too. Ours is the culpability not of the assassin, but of the bystander who takes a snapshot of the murder. Or, when the revolution catches fire, hops on the next plane out.

Sometimes though, just sometimes, I am brought up short by symptoms of my condition. I have never bought a house of any kind, and my ideal domestic environment, I sometimes tell my friends, is a hotel room. I have never voted, or ever wanted to vote, and I eat in restaurants three times a day. I have never supported any nation (in the Olympic games, say) or represented "my country" in anything. Even my name is weirdly international, because my "real name" is one that makes sense only in the home where I have never lived. […]

If I have any deeper home, it is, I suppose, in English. My language is the house I carry around with me as a snail his shell; and in my lesser moments I try to forget that mine is not the language spoken in America, or even, really, by any member of my family.

Yet even here, I find, I cannot place my accent, or reproduce it as I can the tones of others. And I am so used to modifying my English inflections according to whom I'm talking to – an American, an Englishman, a villager in Nepal, a receptionist in Paris – that I scarcely know what kind of voice I have.

I wonder, sometimes, if this new kind of non-affiliation may not be alien to something fundamental in the human state. The refugee at least harbours passionate feelings about the world he has left – and generally seeks to return there; the exile at least is propelled by some kind of strong emotion away from the old country towards the new – indifference is not an exile emotion. But what does the transit lounger feel? What are the issues that we would die for? What are the passions that we would live for?

Vocabulary

4 boarding school (n.): a school where students live as well as study - **8 budget** (adj.): very low in price - **13 scarcely** (adj.): almost not or almost none at all - **18 breed** (n.): a particular kind of person or type - **18 transcontinental** (adj.): crossing a continent - **18 tribe** (n.): a social group consisting of people of the same race - **21 transit lounge** (n.): airport lounge for people who use the airport to switch directly to another flight without leaving the airport - **25 revolving door** (n.): a type of door in the entrance of a large building, which goes around and around as people go through it - **25 impermanent** (adj.): /ɪmˈpɜːmənənt/ not staying the same for ever - **28 unprecedented** (adj.): /ʌnˈpresɪdəntɪd/ never having happened before - **33 internationalism** (n.): the belief that nations should work together and help each other - **45 enchantment** (n.): the quality of being very pleasant or attractive - **55 disembarkation form**: form to be filled out before getting off a ship or airplane - **58 marital status** (n.): /ˈmærɪtl/ whether someone is married - used especially on official forms - **62 deracinated** (adj.): /dɪˈræsəneitɪd/ with one's (cultural) roots removed - **64 ostracism** (n.): /ˈɒstrəsɪzəm/ if a group of people ostracize someone, they refuse to accept them as a member of the group - **65 alight** (v.): to step out of a vehicle after a journey - **65 severed** (adj.): /ˈsevərd/ cut off - **66 citizen** (n.): someone who lives in a particular town, country, or state - **68 alienation** (n.): the feeling of not being part of society or a group - **70 exile** (n.): a person who is forced to leave his or her country and live in another country, especially for political reasons - **70 refugee** (n.): someone who has been forced to leave their country, especially during a war, or for political or religious reasons - **78 playpen** (n.): an enclosed area in which a very small child can play safely, that is like an open box with sides made of bars or a net - **87 savour** (v.): to fully enjoy a time or experience - **91 stirred** (adj.): if a feeling stirs in you, you begin to feel it - **95 juggle** (v.): (here) to try to fit two or more jobs, activities etc into your life, especially with difficulty - **98 affiliation** (n.): the connection or involvement that someone or something has with a political, religious etc organization - **100 accountable** (adj.): responsible for the effects of your actions and willing to explain or be criticized for them - **105 dogma** (n.): a set of firm beliefs held by a group of people who expect other people to accept these beliefs without thinking about them - **106 inexplicable** (adj.): too unusual or strange to be explained or understood - **107 agnostic** (n.): someone who believes that people cannot know whether God exists or not – **107 partisanship** (n.): strongly supporting a particular political party, plan or leader, usually without considering the other choices carefully – **109 fathom** (v.): to understand what something means after thinking about it carefully – **114 non-aligned** (adj.): a non-aligned country does not support, or is not dependent on, any of the powerful countries in the world – **116 self-serving** (adj.): showing that you will only do something if it will gain you an advantage – used to show disapproval – **116 nationalism** (n.): love for your own country and the belief that it is better than any other country – **116 breed** (v.): produce – **118 culpability** (n.): deserving blame – **119 bystander** (n.): someone who watches what is happening without taking part – **124 domestic environment** (n.): relating to family relationships and life at home – **134 snail** (n.): a small soft creature that moves very slowly and has a hard shell on its back – **139 inflection** (n.): the way in which a word changes its form to show a difference in its meaning or use – **141 receptionist** (n.): someone whose job is to welcome and deal with people arriving in a hotel or office building, visiting a doctor etc – **147 propel** (v.): to move, drive, or push something forward

Explanations

48 golden arches: synonym for McDonald's (the yellow M-sign of McDonald's looks like two golden arches) – **54 None of the Above**: Option to be filled out on forms if no other answer fits – **74 Khmer**: tribe of Cambodia – **75 Farsi**: the language of Iran – **80 Kazuo Ishiguro**: (1954-) novelist, born in Nagasaki but came to England in 1960. Well-known for novels such as *The Artist of the Floating World* (1986) and *The Remains of the Day* (1989) – **89 Rabindranath Tagore**: (1861-1941) a Bengali Indian writer, one of the most important Indian writers of the 20th century. His works include *Gitanjali* and *Chitra*, a play which he translated into English. – **93 Salman Rushdie**: (1947-) a British writer born in India, who won the Booker Prize for his novel *Midnight's Children*. In 1988 his novel *The Satanic Verses* offended Muslims because they said that it was insulting to their religion, with the result that Ayatollah Khomeini in Iran gave a *fatwa*, an order that Rushdie should be killed. He had to live in a secret place for many years.

AWARENESS

1   "Mobility" is much in demand in today's job market. Make a list of the advantages and disadvantages of an international career.
2   Would you be willing and able to move around the world as a professional for a large part of your (future) career?

COMPREHENSION

3   Describe Iyer's life as a "global player". What makes it so different from the life of the average person?
4   What advantages of his lifestyle does Iyer mention? Make a list.
5   What disadvantages and problems does he mention? Again, make a list.
6   In Iyer's opinion, do the advantages outweigh the disadvantages?

ANALYSIS

7   Sum up the line of Iyer's article in a short précis.
8   Describe and define the position Iyer has towards globalization.
9   Can you define what it means to be a "nowhere man"?
10 Find synonyms in the text to describe this sort of person. Then decide whether they carry positive or negative connotations for you.
11 With regard to the text, does this sort of person belong to a certain class or social group? Give reasons for your answer.
12 Examine the style which makes this article very deep and reflective.
13 "If all the world is alien to us, all the world is home." Discuss the paradox.
14 Iyer does not "get stirred by the raising of a flag" – what does the author imply here? Do more and more people feel like him?
15 Explain the significance and meaning of the phrase "nationalism breeds monsters, internationalism breeds them too" (lines 116 ff.). What, specifically, are these "monsters"?
16 "My language is the house I carry around with me as a snail his shell." Explain the effects of these words (lines 133 f.). Would you agree?

OPINION

17 Consider Iyer's description of the life of a cosmopolitan. Does it look attractive to you?
18 What are the limits to Iyer's lifestyle? You may want to consider values or things that are important to you, which are not mentioned in the text.

PROJECTS

19 Imagine you had a chance to talk to Iyer. What sort of questions would you ask him?
20 What will your life look like, say, twenty years from now? Write an essay, describing your way of life.

21

Spice up Your Life – International Low-budget Snacks

Are you are looking for a tasty equivalent to what's in your lunchbox? Let's take a look into lunchboxes all over the world (compiled from www.allrecipes.com).

NORTH AMERICA: *Peanut butter sandwich*

Slice of bread, spread 1tbsp. peanut butter on the bottom, spread 1tbsp. of strawberry jam on the top.

Info

Conversion into the metric system of measures:

1 pound (16 ounces)	450 grams
1 ounce	30 grams
1 teaspoon	5 millilitres
1 tablespoon (3 teaspoons)	15 millilitres
1 cup (16 tablespoons)	250 millilitres
1 pint (2 cups)	568 millilitres (USA: 500 ml)
1 quart (4 cups)	1 litre (about)
68 °F	= 20 °C
50 °F	= 10 °C
32 °F	= 0 °C
°C	= 5/9 x (F-32)
1 inch	= 2,54 cm
1 foot	= 12 inches = 30,48 cm
1 mile	= 1,61 km
1 gallon	= 4,5 l (USA: 3,79 l)

SOUTH AMERICA/MEXICO: *Flour tortilla*

Ingredients: 3 cups unbleached flour, 2 tsp. baking powder, 1 tsp. salt, 4-6 tsp. vegetable shortening or lard, 1 1/4 cups warm water.

Recipe: Mix dry ingredients, add shortening, add warm water a little at a time, knead the dough for a few minutes until it is soft but not sticky. Form about 12 small dough balls, let them rest for 10 min. or more. Roll them out fairly thin, lay them in a hot, dry pan and flip after a few seconds. They are ready to be served.

ASIA: *Spring roll*

The Asian word for snack is dim sum, and the spring roll is one of the most popular snacks.

Recipe: Skin: mix 1 cup unbleached flour and 1 tsp. salt, add 2 eggs (beaten) and enough water (about two cups) for a smooth batter. Let rest 20 min., pour 2 tsp. batter in slightly oiled pan, tilting pan to cover entire surface with batter. Turn over and remove to a flat dish.

Filling: Heat peanut oil (1 tbsp.) and stir-fry bean sprouts (1 pound), 3/4 cup bamboo shoots, 1/4 cup water chestnuts, celery (2 ribs), 2 tbsp. soy sauce and 1/2 tsp. sugar for 2 min. Pour off any juices and add 2 tsp. sesame oil, 2 tsp. green onion, 2 tbsp. cornstarch and egg slivers (2 eggs). Cool and place 3 tsp. on edge of spring roll skin, fold skin over twice, fold in sides. Deep fry, seam side down, in hot oil until crisp and golden.

GREAT BRITAIN: *Fish and chips*

Fried potatoes are called chips in British English, while Americans call them French fries (or freedom fries in times of war). Potato chips, an American innovation, are an entirely different food, known as crisps in the UK. Nonetheless, the combination of deep-fried fish in batter and deep-fried potatoes is called fish and chips even in the US.

Recipe: Preheat oven to 450° F. Grease a baking sheet. Cut two peeled potatoes lengthwise into 1 inch french fries. Toss the potatoes with oil, salt and chili powder and arrange them on the baking sheet, turning once in 30 min. Mix bread crumbs, salt, pepper and oregano in a shallow dish. Beat egg whites (2 eggs). Dip the fish strips into the egg whites and then into the bread crumb mixture, taking care to coat the fish on all sides. Heat oil in a pan, fry fish strips about 3–5 min. per side.

AFRICA: *Plaintains*

Plantains, "potatoes of the air" or "cooking bananas", are the fruit of the Musa Paradisiaca, a type of banana plant. Plantains are more starchy than sweet and must be cooked before being eaten. They are a staple crop in much of Africa and are served boiled, steamed, baked, or fried. Plantains grilled over a charcoal fire are popular street food in many African cities.

Recipe: Peel and cut plantains into thin slices. Heat oil in a pan and fry until golden. Serve with a hot sauce or salt as a snack.

AUSTRALIA: *Vegemite sandwich*

Nothing could be more Australian than Vegemite, a sandwich spread. This strange-looking black spread is extremely salty-tasting; it is made by blending brewer's yeasts, one of the richest known sources of B complex vitamins. 22,7 million jars of Vegemite are manufactured in Australia every year.

Suggestion for serving: Thick crusty white bread with Vegemite, tomato cottage cheese and shallots.

Vocabulary

tbsp. (abbr.): a tablespoon full of – **tsp.**: a teaspoon of – **vegetable shortening / lard** (n.): vegetable or animal fat – **knead** (v.): /niːd / to press a mixture of flour and water many times with your hands - **batter** (n) : a mixture of flour, eggs, milk etc, used in cooking and for making bread, cakes etc. – **sprouts** (n.): if vegetables, seeds, or plants sprout, they start to grow, producing shoots, buds, or leaves – **soya sauce** (n) : a dark brown liquid made from soya beans that is used especially in Japanese and Chinese cooking – **corn starch** (n.): corn flour – **sliver** (n.): /ˈslɪvəll 'slɪvər/ a small pointed or thin piece that has been cut or broken off something - **starchy** (adj.), **starch** (n.): a substance which provides your body with energy and is found in foods such as grain, rice, and potatoes, or a food that contains this substance (synonym: carbohydrate) – **staple** (adj.): forming the greatest or most important part of something – **charcoal** (n.): a black substance made of burned wood that can be used as fuel – **shallot** (n.): /ʃəˈlɒt/ a vegetable like a small onion

PROJECTS
1 Now "cook up a storm" and surprise your friends!
2 For further recipes consult: www.allrecipes.com/ and www.vegetarianrecipe.com/.

22

"You Know What They Put on French Fries in Holland?"

Pulp Fiction (1994) is a humorous, but very violent US film directed by Quentin Tarantino, who also wrote the script. Probably the best-known and most-quoted scene in the film is a discussion between Vincent, played by a sleazy John Travolta, and Jules, played by Samuel L. Jackson. On their way to bungle a job as rather unprofessional killers, they discuss food differences around the world. The line "You know what they put on French fries in Holland?" has become almost proverbial to indicate cultural differences – or ignorant attitudes towards them.

1 **VINCENT:** D' you know what the funniest thing about Europe is?

JULES: What?

VINCENT: It's the little differences. A lotta the same 5 shit we got here, they got there, but there they're a little different.

JULES: Examples?

VINCENT: Well, in Amsterdam, you can buy beer in a movie theater. And I don't mean in a paper cup either. 10 They give you a glass of beer, like in a bar. In Paris, you can buy beer at McDonald's. Also, you know what they call a Quarter Pounder with Cheese in Paris?

JULES: They don't call it a Quarter Pounder with Cheese?

VINCENT: No, they got the metric system there, they 15 wouldn't know what a Quarter Pounder is.

JULES: What'd they call it?

VINCENT: Royale with Cheese.

JULES (repeating): Royale with Cheese. What'd they call a Big Mac?

VINCENT: Big Mac's a Big Mac, but they call it Le Big 20 Mac.

JULES: What do they call a Whopper?

VINCENT: I dunno, I didn't go into a Burger King. But you know what they put on French fries in Holland instead of ketchup? 25

JULES: What?

VINCENT: Mayonnaise.

JULES: Goddamn!

VINCENT: I seen 'em do it. And I don't mean a little bit on the side of the plate, they drown 'em in it. 30

JULES: Uucccch!

AWARENESS

1 Does the term "McDonaldization" mean anything to you? What could it signify in the context of globalization?

COMPREHENSION

2 Make sure you understand all the references to fast food in the text. What exactly is the difference between a hamburger at McDonald's and Burger King? Does it matter?

ANALYSIS

3 Describe the colloquialisms of the text. How do they contribute to its humour?

4 What makes this conversation so funny? Think of the contrast between what is said and how it is said.

OPINION

5 Do you sometimes have similar conversations about trivial things? Why do people worry about the difference between Pepsi and Coke, McDonald's and Burger King?

6 What is your opinion on the levelling-out effect of globalization? Will all cultural differences be erased in the end?

23

Legends of Food – the Hamburger and the Pizza

Have you ever wondered where the first hamburger and the first pizza came from? Here are some possible explanations (see also www.hungrymonster.com, http://whatscookingamerica.net, adapted).

(1) Around the year 1885, Charlie Nagreen of Seymour, Wisconsin, at the age of 15 went to a local fair and set up a stand selling meatballs. Business wasn't good and he quickly realised that it was because the meatballs were too difficult to eat. In a flash of innovation, he flattened the meatballs, placed them between two slices of bread and called his creation a hamburger. Hamburger Charlie returned to sell hamburgers at the fair every year until his death in 1951.

(2) Around 1891, Otto Kusaw was a cook in a restaurant on the waterfront in Hamburg, Germany. He made a sandwich that the sailors who stopped at the port liked very much. It was made with thin patties of ground beef sausage fried in butter. A fried egg was placed on top of the meat and then placed between two slices of lightly buttered bread. In 1894, sailors who had been to Hamburg and visited the port of New York, told restaurant owners about Otto's great sandwiches and the restaurants began making the sandwiches for the sailors. It is said that all the sailors had to do was to ask for a "hamburger".

And where is the home of the pizza?

(1) Around the year 1522, tomatoes were brought back to Europe from the New World (Peru). Originally they were thought to be poisonous, but later the poorer people of Naples added the new tomatoes to their yeast dough and created the first simple pizza as we know it. They usually had only flour, olive oil, lard, cheese, and tomatoes with which to feed their families.

(2) In 1889 Umberto I. (1844–1900), King of Italy, and his wife, Queen Margherita di Savoia (1851–1926), were in Naples on holiday and called to their palace the most popular pizzaiolo (pizza chef) to taste his specialities. He prepared three kinds of pizzas: one with pork fat, cheese and basil; one with garlic, oil and tomatoes; and another with mozzarella, basil and tomatoes. The Queen liked one of his specialities so much that she sent to the pizzaiolo a letter to thank him. Raffael Esposito (pizzaiolo) dedicated his speciality to the Queen and called it "Pizza Margherita".

Vocabulary

2 fair (n.): an outdoor market or event – **16 patty** (n.): small, flat piece of cooked meat or other food – **30 yeast** (n.): a type of fungus used for producing alcohol in beer and wine, and for making bread rise – **32 lard** (n.) white fat from pigs that is used in cooking – **37 Naples** (n.): an industrial city and port in southeast Italy – **42 basil** (n.): a strong-smelling and strong-tasting herb used in cooking – **42 garlic** (n.): a plant like a small onion, used in cooking to give a strong taste – **46 dedicate** (v.): say that it has been made for someone that you love or respect

AWARENESS
1 What sort of restaurants are there in your area? Make a survey (for example from the telephone book).
2 Do you know how food in foreign restaurants you have been to compares with the cuisine in their country of origin?
3 Why have doner kebab in Germany and chicken tikka masala in England become so very popular?

COMPREHENSION
4 Retell each legend of food in one or two short sentences.

ANALYSIS
5 Why do legends like these exist? What do they tell us about the origin of food or dishes?

OPINION
6 What are the reasons for different traditions in cooking?
7 Does food reflect cultural habits? Why and how?

PROJECT
8 Find out more about national and international dishes at www.recipeland.com.

24 The Onion and the Iceberg – Culture and the Individual

Intercultural competence has been one of the buzz words used in teaching foreign languages and cultures in the last decades. It means learning more than language skills, rather acquiring a number of competencies which include the awareness of cultural differences with regard to perceptions of time, space, politeness, power, nature, etc. The culturally competent person acts with a great degree of self-reflexivity and cultural awareness of differences. He or she shows flexibility and tolerance in cross-cultural encounters. For a start, it is helpful to think about culture(s) in general and to become aware of national stereotypes. A list of Do's and Don'ts for the country one visits might also be helpful. However, any intercultural exchange – like any human exchange – is always very complex and cannot be based on a simple set of rules.

Info

Critical Incidents

Skills in cross-cultural or intercultural communication can be achieved by thinking about or possibly acting out "critical incidents". What, for example, do the following situations reveal about culturally different concepts of eye contact, directness in speech and personal space?

A British student on an exchange programme in Berlin complains about being stared at on the underground train. "They stare at me straight in the face as if I've come from Mars", she says.

A German manager working in Thailand is unhappy that his secretary regularly arrives at work at least 30 minutes, and sometimes as much as one hour, late for work. One morning when she arrives he explodes in front of the others in the busy office. The next day she hands in her resignation.

A German guest professor in the USA keeps his office door closed and is surprised that very few students come to see him. He wonders if the Americans reject him because he is German. He is especially irritated one day when he finds out that the students have stuck a sign on the door saying 'Beware of the Dog'.

(Adapted from Robert Gibson, *Intercultural Business Communication*, Berlin: Cornelsen, 2000, 38, 43, 50.)

*C*ulture...

is like an Onion

1 Culture is like an onion: it has many layers, which we need to peel away to understand the individual at the centre. When we talk about com-
5 munication with people from different cultures, we usually think of communication with different countries. But countries form simply the outside
10 layer of the culture onion. Regions, religions, class, gender, race, etc. within a country are often as varied as the countries themselves.

At the centre we find individuals who
15 have their own "culture", usually called personality or identity. Often, individual personalities are very different from the national stereotypes we have in our minds. How can we develop the competencies for understanding and responding to these various layers
20 when dealing with people from other countries? One approach would be to build a framework into which cultural experiences can fit. Apart from time, space, politeness, 25 etc. some of the key dimensions of this framework are stereotypes and how we deal with them.

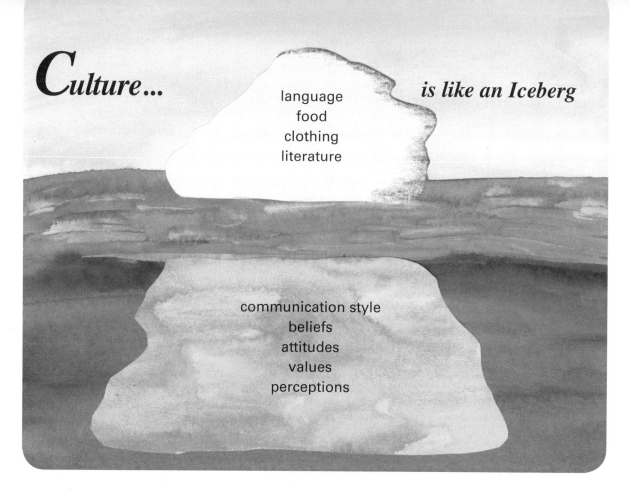

Culture... is like an Iceberg

language
food
clothing
literature

communication style
beliefs
attitudes
values
perceptions

Culture is like an iceberg. Only the tip of the iceberg is visible – in this case expressions of culture like language, food, clothing, literature, films, etc.

Below the water are the underlying attitudes, beliefs, values and meanings – much more difficult to perceive, detect and define.

Source: Robert Gibson, Intercultural Business Communication *(Berlin: Cornelsen, 2000), 15–18.*

AWARENESS

1 When you were abroad, did you observe different attitudes towards time, space, nature, etc. and how this was expressed in verbal and non-verbal behaviour? Discuss some cultural differences. The first step towards intercultural competence is often to become aware of differences.

COMPREHENSION

2 Think of all the "layers" that are around a person from your country. Make a rough list of them.
3 What else is below the water in the iceberg model? Again, make a list.

ANALYSIS

4 What is left of the self, if culture is like an onion? What makes a person different from others?

OPINION

5 Make a sketch of an onion. Then write down in key expressions what layers make up your culture and your personality.
6 What, in your culture, would be extremely difficult to understand for a foreigner? Brainstorm and make a list. Then discuss and compare your list with those of others.

PROJECT

7 Find out more about intercultural competence by consulting websites on the net. Google "critical incidents".

25

A Very Critical Incident: Three on a Desert Island
(A Satire)

In intercultural competence classes and seminars, students often learn about culturally critical incidents, such as having to express in a polite and inoffensive manner that you need to go to the toilet, that the food you are being served is indigestible, etc. (see page 57). The following scenario is merely fictitious, of course, yet it allows reflections on national stereotypes on a global scale, including the aspect of gender. (From various internet sources, e.g. www.podys.com.)

1 The setting is a group of small tropical islands which are far away from other places and have no people living on them. On these beautiful islands in the middle of the ocean, the following people are suddenly stranded:
5 • Two Italian men and one Italian woman
• Two French men and one French woman
• Two German men and one German woman
• Two Greek men and one Greek woman
• Two English men and one English woman
10 • Two Bulgarian men and one Bulgarian woman
• Two Japanese men and one Japanese woman
• Two Chinese men and one Chinese woman
• Two American men and one American woman
• Two Irish men and one Irish woman

15 Question: What will happen on each island? Make an intelligent guess. Then, but only then, read on.

One month later on these absolutely stunning deserted islands in the middle of nowhere, the following things have occurred:

20 • One Italian man killed the other Italian man for the Italian woman.
• The two French men and the French woman are living happily together in a ménage-à-trois.
• The two German men have a strict weekly schedule
25 of alternating visits with the German woman.
• The two Greek men are sleeping with each other and the Greek woman is cleaning and cooking for them.
• The two English men are waiting for someone to introduce them to the English woman.
30 • The two Bulgarian men take one long look at the endless ocean and another long look at the Bulgarian woman and start swimming.

• The two Japanese have faxed Tokyo and are awaiting instructions.
• The two Chinese men have set up a pharmacy / liquor 35 store / restaurant / laundry and have gotten the woman pregnant in order to supply employees for their store.
• The two American men are contemplating the virtues of suicide, because the American woman keeps on complaining about her body, the true nature of femi- 40 nism, how she can do everything they can do, the necessity of fulfillment, the equal division of household chores, how sand and palm trees make her look fat, how her last boyfriend respected her opinion and treated her nicer than they do, and how her relation- 45 ship with her mother is improving, and how at least the taxes are low and it isn't raining.
• The two Irish men have divided the island into North and South and have set up a distillery. They do not remember if sex is in the picture because it gets sort 50 of foggy after the first few litres of coconut whisky. But they're satisfied because at least the English aren't having any fun.

Vocabulary

17 stunning (adj.): extremely attractive or beautiful – **23 ménage-à-trois**: (French) a sexual relationship involving three people who live together – **24 schedule** (n.): /ˈskedʒʊəl, ˈʃedjuːl/ plan – **25 alternating visits**: one visits one day, the other the next; this pattern continues – **37 employee** (n.): worker – **38 contemplate** (v.): consider, think about it seriously for a period of time – **38 virtue** (n.): (here) advantage, good side – **42 division** (n.): the act of separating something into two or more different parts – **42 household chores**: things to be done in a household, like washing the dishes – **49 distillery** (n.): a factory where strong alcoholic drinks such as whisky are produced

---

TASK

Look at each case individually. Which cultural contexts are alluded to, and which national stereotypes are displayed? What makes the examples funny?

26

Do's and Don'ts – Exploring the World of Social Graces

In books on intercultural competence as well as on the internet you will find many lists with "Do's and Don'ts" – how to behave adequately and what to avoid in a certain culture. It is always recommended to check these lists twice, for some of them may suggest an all-too-simple path towards easy communication, while others are just wrong. Consider the following lists, focusing on the world of social graces. They have been compiled from various sources on the internet.

NORTH AMERICA

Do's:

- Be punctual and never be the last one to leave
- Women first when entering a restaurant

Don'ts:

- It is regarded as extremely rude not to listen to women
- Never walk in front of a woman
- Body hair, especially under the armpits, is deemed vulgar in women

JAPAN

Do's:

- It is usual to bow to "superiors", the younger to the older, at an angle of 30 degrees. But if Europeans don't quite manage that, a lesser pitch is acceptable

Don'ts:

- Never blurt things out straight away
- Avoid direct eye contact and physical contact
- In both Japan and Korea, any form of physical contact during the greeting is improper

ARAB COUNTRIES

Do's:

- Hands often remain clasped a little longer than the greeting while a few personal words are exchanged
- Arabs show their appreciation of food by slurping and belching

Don'ts:

- In Saudi-Arabia, women are excluded from driving cars themselves
- It is dishonouring for an Arab to be touched by an "infidel"
- Never eat with your left hand
- Arab business people are reluctant and unwilling to discuss money

Vocabulary

social graces: good and polite behaviour towards other people – **pitch** (n.): a strong level of feeling about something or a high level of an activity or a quality – **blurt out** (v.): to say something suddenly and without thinking, usually because you are nervous or excited – **slurp** (v.): /slɜːp/ to make a noisy sucking sound while drinking a liquid – **belch** (v.): /beltʃ/ let air from your stomach come out loudly through your mouth – **dishonour** (v.): to make your family, country, profession, etc. lose the respect of other people – **infidel** (n.): /ˈɪnfɪdəl/ an offensive word for someone who has a different religion from you – **reluctant** (adj.): /rɪˈlʌktənt/ slow and unwilling

AWARENESS

1 Make a list of Do's and Don'ts for your own country.
2 What else would you recommend to a foreigner visiting your country?

COMPREHENSION

3 Which of the recommendations have you heard of before?
4 Are these recommendations also true for your country?
5 Are some very obvious? If yes, why would they still be on such a list?
6 Add more Do's and Don'ts to the lists, if you can. Ask people who have already been to these countries.

ANALYSIS

7 What do these recommendations reveal about the cultural background of the person who wrote them down?

OPINION

8 Are these lists helpful to you?
9 What other lists would you like to have (politeness etc.)?

PROJECTS

10 Look at the following examples of culture-specific behaviour. Find out why people in these countries behave that way.

   a) Why are Asians shocked when you sit down and expose the soles of your shoes or feet?
   b) Why do Asians feel disgusted when you touch them with your left hand?
   c) Why do religious Muslim women seem to be searching for something on the street before them?
   d) Why do Asians dislike being hugged or patted on the head, even if this is meant as a gesture of affection?

11 Food, the topic of units 21–23, and communication are often connected, for example in idiomatic expressions. Find out what the following idiomatic expressions mean. Do not look at the solution below first.

   A piece of cake / spill the beans / cry over spilled milk / cream of the crop / fishy / cool as a cucumber / hot potato / put all one's eggs in one basket / the icing on the cake / break the ice

   Solutions (same order):
   • Very easy to do
   • To tell a secret
   • To be upset about something that has already happened and can't be changed
   • The best there is
   • When something seems to be wrong; probably not the truth
   • Has a lot of self-confidence; in perfect control of a situation
   • A topic that causes controversy
   • To depend completely on one thing or one action in order to be successful
   • Something which makes a good situation or activity even better
   • To say or do something which makes people feel less nervous

27 Polly Toynbee

"Who's Afraid of Global Culture?"

Polly Toynbee is a journalist, broadcaster and columnist for the British quality newspaper *The Guardian*. In the following excerpt from her article "Who's Afraid of Global Culture?" she tackles three of the major issues of globalization: Globalization as Americanization, globalization as the spread of Western cultural values, and, finally, the spread of an American-style free market system throughout the world. – The article was published in Will Hutton, Anthony Giddens (eds.), *Global Capitalism*. New York: The New Press, 2000, 191–222 (here 195f., 201).

1 There may be a great conspiracy to Americanise the planet, a Coca-Cola push into remotest corners, but there's no doubt it is often greeted with a warm welcome, creating just as strong a pull to suck more of it in.
5 (Remember trips behind the Iron Curtain and how everyone begged for jeans or any artefact that symbolised the West.) For them the clash of cultures is a draw, but for Westerners it can make us ashamed. Visit a popular holiday resort in the Gambia or in Kenya and you find
10 yourself staying in enclaves that are perfect little replicas of life in Florida plonked down in the midst of such poverty that the schoolchildren, carrying water home for miles, stop to beg for old biros outside the heavily guarded hotel compound gates. The hotel probably uses
15 more electricity than the whole surrounding district. No holiday is better designed to make Westerners feel their own lives to be greedy, idle, rich and wasteful in comparison, though infinitely desirable to those denied it.

Naturally they want more of what we have got.
20 Cultural globalisation for them means seizing the opportunity to have our wealthy life-style, even if, sadly, a baseball cap is as much as they can get their hands on. It may be relatively easy for the Taliban or the Iranians at their strictest to stop this Western filth
25 crossing their borders, to ban television and every outward sign of decadence. But they know the real battle is in the hearts and minds of their own people: unless ruthlessly suppressed by culture police, people can't be trusted to watch Western television.
30 Why? Is it just the cry of poverty for more wealth? Often no doubt it is, though something more important may lie beneath. In the artefacts of the West they glimpse not just a world of plenty, but of freedom and opportunity – the American dream symbolised in the
35 baseball cap. It may be dangerous folly for we know how savage Western society is and what the West has done to exploit and destroy native and alien cultures everywhere. Western 'freedom' traditionally tends to arrive as it does to the Yanomami in the rain forest – in
40 the form of hired killers and bulldozers. Some dream.

But for many others the dream is real enough: opportunity lies in the West even if you have to swim there. Those harmonious village communities can be stifling with their rigid hierarchies and an immutable social predestination for every baby born. Getting 45 away may be dangerous and lead to much worse, but the wide world still beckons seductively, every ancient fairy story starting with boys setting out to seek their fortune.

We are selective in our feelings about global culture. 50 We may regret the Coca-Cola bottles but we will strive with missionary fervour to spread our most important values. In our political and social culture we have a democratic way of life which we know, without any doubt at all, is far better than any other in the history of 55 humanity.

Deeply flawed maybe, but the best so far, Western liberal democracy is the only system yet devised that maximises freedom for the many. We preach and struggle to practise a doctrine of freedom for women 60 and multicultural optimism – by no means perfect, but probably the best there is. Modern urban society may sometimes be frighteningly free, alienating and lonely, but (for those above abject poverty) it offers a welcome escape from social pressure, superstition, patriarchy 65 and hierarchy. […]

"Another Starbucks on Venus."

However, there are aspects of cultural globalisation that we should and can resist. Proud though we may be of freedom and democracy, too often it comes linked to a culture of the rampant free market and economic theories entirely predicated on insatiable greed. We deliberately encourage the greed ethos everywhere in order to create new markets, only lending money to those who profess to share our belief in it. Western economies only know how to grow or die, over-producing and over-consuming without any concept of satiety.

With shameless triumphalism at the end of the Cold War the West sent in nothing but the hard culture of Thatcherism which has brought the former USSR to its knees, allowing privateering banditry to run riot. Worse still, it has risked the reputation of liberal capitalism and democracy with a disillusioned people. The unfettered market is not the best ambassador of freedom, unmitigated by real human rights ideals or softened by the policies with which we ourselves regulate and tame it at home. The communist world discovered you can't have a thriving competitive economy without political freedom – but the West knows it is also difficult to control the worst savagery of the free market within a politically free system.

Vocabulary

6 artefact (n.): an object such as a tool, weapon etc that was made in the past and is historically important - **7 draw** (n.): a fight ends in a draw if neither party has won - **10 enclave** (n.): /ˈenkleɪv/ a small area that is within a larger area where people of a different kind or nationality live - **10 replica** (n.): /ˈreplɪkə/ an exact copy of something, especially a building, a gun, or a work of art - **11 plonk down** (v.): put something down somewhere, especially in a noisy and careless way - **14 compound** (n.): an area that contains a group of buildings and is surrounded by a fence or wall - **44 stifling** (adj.): /ˈstaɪflɪŋ/ a situation that is stifling stops you from developing your own ideas and character - **44 immutable social predestination**: society has prearranged the individual's course of life right from his or her birth - **47 beckon** (n.): call - **52 fervour** (n.): /ˈfɜːvə/ very strong belief or feeling - **60 doctrine** (n.): a set of beliefs that form an important part of a religion or system of ideas - **65 patriarchy** (n.): social system in which men have all the power - **70 rampant** (adj.): if something bad, such as crime or disease, is rampant, there is a lot of it and it is very difficult to control - **71 predicated on insatiable greed**: based on greed which will never be satisfied - **76 satiety** (n.): (rare) having satisfied a desire or need for something such as food or sex, especially so that you feel you have had too much - **77 triumphalism** (n.): behaviour which shows that someone is too proud of their success and too pleased about the defeat of their opponents; used to show disapproval - **80 allowing privateering banditry to run riot**: allowing rampant and brutal capitalism to spread without any checks - **82 unfettered** (adj.) not restricted by laws or rules - **83 unmitigated** (adj.): sth. that is completely bad or good - **85 tame** (v.): reduce the power or strength of something and prevent it from causing trouble - **87 thriving** (adj.): /ˈθraɪvɪŋ/ a thriving company, business etc is very successful

Explanations

79 Thatcherism: The general principles on which Margaret Thatcher's government was based when she was Prime Minister of the UK, especially her ideas about economic management. Her ideas, which have become known as Thatcherism, have also influenced politicians in other countries. She reduced taxes, took away power from trade unions, and started a programme of privatization (= selling state-owned services such as electricity, gas, and the telephone service, so that they became private companies). Similar terms are Reaganomics (referring to the former US president Ronald Regan), laissez-faire capitalism, neo-liberalism, etc.

AWARENESS

1 Mahatma Gandhi, the great Indian politician, once stated: "Western civilization? I think it would be a good idea." What did he imply by this remark?

COMPREHENSION

2 Why, according to the author, is Westernization "greeted with a warm welcome" (l. 3) in many developing countries?

3 Why, according to the author, do we feel uneasy about this?

4 What is the best the West "exports" to other countries?

5 What, on the contrary, is the worst the West spreads across the globe?

ANALYSIS

6 Divide the text into sections and write down a key phrase for each section.

7 Outline the main argument of the article in a summary of about five to six sentences.

8 What, according to the article, is the significance of an American baseball cap to non-Americans? As a symbol, what does it stand for? Make a short list from the text.

9 What exactly is the author's view on globalization? In your answer refer to her opinion on cultural and social values as well as on economic concepts.

OPINION

10 Comment on the author's attitude towards what the West has to offer for other countries. Do you find her opinion convincing?

11 Are there alternatives to the spread of free market economies? If yes, describe them.

28 | Angela Merkel

Opening Address at the World Economic Forum on 24 January 2007 in Davos

Angela Merkel was born in Hamburg in 1954. In 2005, the Christian Democratic Union (CDU) won the federal election and she became the Chancellor of Germany. (She was re-elected for four more years in September 2009.) In her Opening Address at the World Economic Forum in Davos, which she originally held in German, she talked about the advantages, disadvantages, and consequences of globalization from a politician's perspective. – Angela Merkel, "Opening Address at the World Economic Forum in Davos, 24 January 2007", Translation/transcript, https://members.weforum.org/pdf/AM_2007/merkel.pdf.

1 The challenge in this is that old habits, perquisites and inherited rights no longer guarantee success. The old hierarchies are being flattened. As the American journalist Thomas Friedman has said, the world is flat.
5 Resources, potentials and power can shift completely overnight. […] Nonetheless this […] also highlights the downside of globalization. Hope for one side means worry and fear for the others. We politicians know these concerns only too well and we must
10 therefore do all we can to shape globalization in political terms. We must not neglect this aspect because people look to us and ask what we are doing to give globalization a human face. […]

This means that dealing with the consequences of
15 globalization is above all an intellectual challenge, not least for Europeans. During the past 200 years we, and indeed Europe as a whole, became accustomed to taking a highly Eurocentric view of the world. Today we see that this simple view no longer applies. […]

Would it not be a successful strategy to exploit our 20 strengths ruthlessly, secure the global resources necessary for our own prosperity just in time, and build a few walls to conceal our own weaknesses? My short and sweet answer is no. I'm firmly convinced that the process of globalization is one of liberalization 25 because, as Benjamin Franklin, one of America's Founding Fathers, once said, "those who would give up essential Liberty, to purchase a little temporary Safety, deserve neither Liberty nor Safety."

Vocabulary

1 **perquisite** (n.): (fml.) s.th. that you can get legally from your work in addition to your wages, such as goods, meals, or a car – 2 **inherit** (v.): to receive money, property etc from s.o. after they have died – 3 **flatten** (v.): to make s.th. flat or flatter – 5 **shift** (v.): to move from one place or position to another – 7 **downside** (n.): the negative part or disadvantage of s.th. – 11 **neglect** (v.): to pay too little attention to s.th. – 17 **accustomed to** (adj.): to be familiar with s.th.

and accept it as normal – 20 **exploit** (v.): to use s.th. fully and effectively – 21 **ruthlessly** (adv.): determined and firm when making unpleasant decisions – 22 **prosperity** (n.): when people have money and everything that is needed for a good life – 23 **conceal** (v.): hide – 28 **purchase** (v.): (fml.) to buy s.th. – 29 **deserve** (v.): to have earned s.th. by good or bad actions or behaviour

1 What does Chancellor Merkel allude to when she speaks out against "building walls"?
2 Do you share Chancellor Merkel's opinions?

GENERAL TASKS

Choose one of the following tasks:
1 Basing your information on the texts read so far, write a dialogue between an opponent and a supporter of globalization.
2 Use what you have learnt in this book (and any other information you can obtain) to put together a report on globalization which you would like to present as an oral report of 30 minutes.
3 Try to make a list of the main points you have learnt about globalization in this book. Which of them are relevant for you?
4 Make a list of the pros and cons of globalization. What is the bottom line for you? Do you see it as a threat, challenge, or opportunity?

Competence Training

You can use this *Viewfinder* volume to practise most or all of the skills you will need to satisfy the requirements set out in the European Frame of Reference (up to level C1) and tested in exams like the German *Abitur* (all *Bundesländer*), TOEFL or IELTS. Details about all the skills (often referred to in German as *Kompetenzen*) that you can work to improve and which of the texts and/or sections from the book will be most useful in doing it are set out on these pages. They provide cross-references to the Viewfinder Reference Library (where you can find out exactly how to do things). You will get the RL from your teacher or you can download it from http://www.langenscheidt.de. At the end there is a revision checklist to make sure you can remember the main points the book deals with. This can be used for exam revision.

Language Skills

Basic and advanced language skills	Oral skills	Written skills
• grammar/structure • vocabulary (new words, word formation) • idiom • register	• pronunciation • intonation • presentation	• spelling • punctuation • text layout

All the texts in this book can help you practise and extend your competence in the active language skills of **speaking** and **writing** and the receptive skills of **reading** and **listening**. You should have learnt the basic language skills in English before you started working with this book. If you're not very confident yet, don't worry. You'll be able to practice all these skills and bring them up to a more advanced level working with any of the texts here. Some of the tasks are better for oral skills and others for written skills. Try to learn new words in their contexts (without trying to find the equivalent in your own language), and note down points which give you trouble, concentrating on learning them and checking your work specially to make sure you don't make the same mistake again. You will find a lot of helpful material in the Reference Library.

Speaking
- ability to pronounce English correctly (using correct accent and intonation)
- ability to use different idioms and registers
- managing discourse (making an appropriate choice of vocabulary, sentence structure, rhetorical devices, text structure) in, for example, everyday conversation or presentations

Listening
- comprehension of content
- ability to understand a variety of spoken text types (unscripted conversations, discussions; scripted news broadcasts, talks, speeches)
- being aware of rhetorical devices used by speakers
- ability to understand different social and geographical accents and dialects

Reading
- comprehension of content
- understanding of a writer's train of thought
- ability to recognize and understand a variety of text types, fictional and non-fictional

Writing
- ability to spell and punctuate correctly
- ability to write a number of different text types (essay, letter, report, presentation, commentary, analysis) using the appropriate vocabulary, grammar and text structure.

Don't forget: you can learn from mistakes, but repeated mistakes are a waste of time. The more proficient your English is, the more fun it is to use, and the better impression it will make on your communication partners.

Text Types

This volume contains the following types of non-fictional and fictional texts which you will be asked to analyse:

Non-fictional texts

survey of facts	texts 1, 7, 26
expository text / quotes	introduction (4–7)
political speech	text 28
newspaper article	texts 8, 12, 13, 20, 27
monograph (excerpt)	texts 3, 6, 9, 11, 17
internet presence	texts 10, 15
recipe	text 21

Fictional texts

novel (excerpt)	texts 4, 18, 19
short story	text 16
movie dialogue	text 22
joke	text 25

Visual texts

chart, graph, diagram	texts 6, 17, 21
photograph	texts 1, 6, 9, 10, 11, 12, 16, 18, 19, 21, 23, 24, 27
cartoon	texts 1 (p. 10), 5 (18), 11 (29), 12 (32, 33), 27
illustration	introduction (p. 7), text 24 (58)
timeline	text 1
book cover	texts 17, 19
painting	text 4
poster	text 15 (37)
screenshot	text 22
map	text 2
graph	texts 2, 5, 15
statistics	texts 14, 15, 17

Particular study skills when approaching texts

The tasks and questions which follow each text are designed to develop skills and competences in a number of areas: language practice and understanding, analyzing and appreciating a wide variety of fictional and non-fictional texts. The tasks will also enable you to develop your own ideas on the topics dealt with, and motivate you to carry out further research into areas that interest you.

AWARENESS:

Before reading a text you should be aware of certain ideas, facts, expectations or prejudices which form the context of the text itself. A skill to practice in all texts is:
Note taking; this is a key skill for
a) preparing for discussions and
b) reading and analysing texts (see below)

Other skills to practise here include:

COLLECTING AND COLLATING IDEAS:

brainstorming (RL B 2)	texts 2 (2, 4, 5), 3 (1, 3, 4, 8), 4 (2, 3), 5 (2, 3), 6 (2, 6), 7 (2), 8 (1, 2), 9 (1, 2), 10 (1), 11 (1, 7, 15, 17), 12 (1, 4, 5, 8), 13 (1, 4), 15 (1, 2), 16 (1, 2, 8), 17 (2, 9), 18 (2), 19 (1, 2, 4, 15), 20 (3, 8–10, 19), 24 (5, 6), 26 (1, 2, 5, 6)
making lists	texts 3 (2), 6 (4, 8, 9, 26), 7 (1, 6), 12 (2, 13), 16 (4), 17 (2, 4), 19 (10), 20 (1, 4, 5), 24 (2, 3, 6), 27 (8), 28 (3, 4)

question and answer session	texts 1 (2, 3), 2 (1), 6 (7, 10), 7 (1, 2), 8 (3–6, 9), 9 (2, 3), 11 (2–5, 8, 11, 18, 19), 12 (3, 6, 7, 9–11), 13 (2), 15 (3, 6), 16 (3–7, 9, 10, 13), 17 (3, 5, 7, 8, 10), 18 (3–7), 19 (5, 6, 8, 9, 11, 12–14, 16), 20 (6, 11, 15), 22 (2–4), 23 (5), 24 (4), 26 (3, 7), 27 (2–5, 9)
reports on individual experience	introduction (7), 3 (1, 4), 5 (1, 7), 6 (1, 3, 19, 24), 9 (1), 17 (1, 13), 18 (1, 4), 23 (1, 2), 24 (1), 28 (tasks 4, general tasks 5)
general discussions	introduction (1), 1 (7, 8), 2 (3, 7), 4 (4–8), 5 (5–7) (p. 18 3, 5), 6 (11–14, 19–23, 27), 7 (5), 8 (9), 9 (5, 10, 11), 10 (3), 11 (6, 9, 12–14, 20), 12 (12, 13; p. 33: 1–4), 13 (5, 6), 14 (1), 15 (6, 7), 16 (14–18), 17 (11–13), 18 (8, 9, 11), 19 (17–21), 20 (2, 13, 14, 16–18), 22 (1, 5, 6), 23 (3, 6, 7), 24 (6), 25 (task), 26 (4, 8, 9), 27 (1, 10, 11), 28 (tasks 1, 2)
practical research	texts 1 (4, 6, 9), 3 (10–13), 4 (1), 5 (4, 9), 10 (3), 12 (2), 14 (1), 15 (8), 16 (19), 21 (1), 24 (7), 26 (6, 10, 11)
internet research	texts 4 (9), 5 (9), 8 (10), 10 (2), 11 (16), 12 (14), 14 (2), 16 (20, 21), 18 (10), 19 (22, 24, 25), 21 (2), 23 (8), 28 (project)
role play	text 6 (26)

During Reading You Can Practice a Number of Skills:

- skimming for general impressions
- scanning to find out facts or information
- note-making (RL A 4)
- marking important passages
- deducing meanings from context
- using a monolingual dictionary (RL A 3)
- using a bilingual dictionary (RL A 3)
- dividing the text
- summarizing (RL C 3)
- finding the deeper meaning
- appreciating aesthetic qualities

In this *Viewfinder* you can practice all these skills on any text. Usually, apart from skimming, you will need to read a text at least three times. The questions under the heading 'Comprehension' are designed for the first seven skills on the list; the 'Analysis' questions will help you practice the last four skills.

After reading:

After you have read the text there are 'Analysis' and 'Opinion' questions to help you discover more meaning in the text, and think about what it means for you personally or what its implications are. You can do these questions alone, in pairs or groups, or as a class. You can answer them individually, present your answers to a plenum, or present them in writing.

Individual answers can be in the form of clearly organized notes or an essay.
Individual written answers can be in the form of a presentation based on notes.
Make sure your answers are clear and concise and relevant.
Check that your listeners have understood your answer.

Answers can also be produced orally or in writing in pair-work or group-work. This will enable you to practise the following teamwork skills:
- using the opportunity of practising English without being supervised
- organizing and dividing up tasks
- co-operating and pooling ideas and skills
- using appropriate research tools
- practising time-management skills (keeping to a timetable)
- choosing an appropriate type of presentation
- using media as presentation aids.

The 'Opinion' questions can be used for various forms of discussion, argument or debate and to practise oral communication skills (see RL B 2). The following tasks are particularly suitable: introduction (6, 7), texts 1 (7, 8), 2 (4, 5), 3 (7, 8), 4 (6–8), 5 (7, 8), 6 (19–24), 7 (5), 8 (1, 2, 8, 9), 9 (10, 11), 11 (12–15), 12 (12), 13 (4), 15 (6, 7), 16 (14–18), 17 (11–13), 18 (8, 9), 19 (17–20), 20 (17, 18), 22 (5, 6), 23 (6, 7), 24 (6), 26 (8, 9), 27 (10, 11), 28 (2)

Textual Analysis Skills

The text analysis questions form the core of your coursework in the *Oberstufe*; their aim is to help you
a) work out what meanings the text might have for you and other readers
b) discover how the text affects you and the means used to achieve this
c) make judgments and write about the content of the text, its value, and its relevance to you.

NON-FICTIONAL TEXTS:

establishing types of text (RL C 1.2.1)	e.g. political speech: text 28; monograph (excerpt): texts 3, 6, 9, 11, 17; newspaper article: texts 8, 12, 20, 27; internet presence: texts 10, 15; recipes: text 21
content (fact v. opinion etc.) (RL C 1.2.1)	texts 3 (3), 6 (6–11, 13, 15–17), 8 (4–6, 9–11), 9 (3–6, 8, 9), 10 (1), 11 (3–11), 12 (3, 4, 6–8, 11), 13 (7), 15 (4), 17 (2–10), 20 (3–11, 14–16), 27 (2–5, 7–9)
structure and form (RL C 1.21)	texts 3 (5), 6 (5), 8 (2, 5, 6), 9 (6, 7), 13 (3, 4), 27 (6)
function (RL C 1.2.2)	texts 6 (15, 15, 18), 8 (3, 10, 12), 9 (7–9), 10 (1), 11 (7), 12 (9–11), 15 (5), 17 (8, 9), 20 (13, 16), 28 (1)
style and tone (RL C 1.2.2) recognizing humor and irony	texts 3 (5), 6 (12, 16), 8 (12), 11 (6), 13 (5), 20 (12)
integrating visual components	introduction (p. 6, 7: 3, 5), texts 4, 10 (1), 12 (1, 2)

FICTIONAL TEXTS:

genre (RL C 1.1)	novel excerpts: texts 4, 18, 19; movie dialogue: text 22; short story: text 16; cartoon: texts 1 (p. 10), 5 (p. 18), 12 (p. 32, 33)
theme (RL C 1.1)	texts 4 (3, 4, 6, 7), 5 (p. 18: 4, 5), 16 (13, 17, 18), 18 (3, 5, 6), 19 (10–13), 22 (1, 6), 25 (task)
character and characterization (RL C 1.1)	texts 5 (p. 18: 2), 16 (11)
setting and atmosphere (RL C 1.1)	texts 16 (3, 4, 12), 19 (4), 22 (2)
structure and formal aspects (RL C 1.1)	texts 5 (p. 18: 4), 16 (8–10), 19 (3)
style (RL C 1.1) / tone (RL C.1)	texts 5 (p. 18: 3), 12 (p. 32: 5; p. 33: 1, 2), 18 (6, 7), 19 (14, 15), 22 (3, 4)

Listening Comprehension Skills

Any of the texts can be used for listening comprehension if you listen to someone reading them, make notes and answer questions or summarise the text. In this context, speeches are particularly relevant because they are delivered publicly and the intonation will often imply the speaker's overall goal. Watching film scenes will also test listening comprehension skills. If the speaker is a non-native speaker of English (e.g. a first generation immigrant to the U.S.), his pronunciation and intonation may differ from standard American English.

Texts that are particularly useful in this context are: texts 19, 22, 28

Visual Text Comprehension Skills

reading cartoons	texts 1, p. 10 (1), 5, p. 18 (1–5), 11 (20), 12 (5, p. 33 1, 2)
analyzing photographs	text 10 (1)
analyzing films	text 22 (3, 4)
analyzing graphs, maps, statistics	texts 2 (2, 3), 14, 15 (3), 17 (11)

Particular Writing Skills / Creative Writing Skills

that you can practice in 'Projects' or on the whole text:

essay	any text (esp. 20 (20))
letter (to editor)	text 8 (16)
statement	introduction (8)
timeline	text 1 (9)
book review	text 6 (25)
book report	text 9 (12)
summary	text 27 (7)
précis	text 20 (7)
dialogue	text 28 (general tasks 1)
report	texts 8 (10), 28 (general tasks 2)

Intercultural Skills

Intercultural linguistic skills: When you use another language you need intercultural skills. Languages differ fundamentally in the ways they express thoughts, or even sometimes in the thoughts they choose to express. So there is no such thing as word-for-word translation. Just think, e.g., of the differences between the German word *fahren* and the English *drive*. Or where you might write: "Mit diesem Bild will der Autor die Unmenschlichkeit des Krieges ausdrücken," in English we might say "The author uses this image to express the horrors of war."

So when working with this book you need to develop skills in relation to the use of the foreign language:
- **Intercultural linguistic awareness:** e.g. seeing how differently words and structures are used in English from their 'equivalents' in your language;
- **Intercultural linguistic competence:** e.g. being able to use the foreign language in the way that members of that language community use it;
- **Register and tone:** e.g. being able to recognize and use different registers like academic or colloquial, or different tones like serious, humorous or sarcastic.

All the texts in this volume expect you to work in the medium of English, which will help you to practice these skills. Specifically, you may be required to actively use various types of equivalents between English and your own language. This will involve the following skills:
- **Translation** (German: *Übersetzung*): Here you must find the nearest possible written equivalent in the other language while making sure that it reads like an original text in terms of structure, idiom, register and tone. This is particularly difficult in literary texts where you have to think of the aesthetic effect as well.
- **Interpreting** (German: *dolmetschen*): As an interpreter you must try to give the nearest equivalent possible of someone's spoken words, either after they have said them, or simultaneously.
- **Conveying the sense** (German: *Mediation*): People may want to know the sense, or message, of a document. They need to know the important facts and figures, but the particular linguistic expressions used in the original are irrelevant.

The texts (or extracts from them) in this *Viewfinder* volume most suitable for translating or conveying the sense are 1, 2, 9, 12, 14. You could also convey the sense of particular positions, like those of the speakers in texts 2, 3 or 13. For a real challenge you could try to translate 4, 6 or 7.

This *Viewfinder* volume *The Global Village* deals with numerous aspects of globalization and living in the global village. It focuses on different cultures, and so it is particularly useful for practicing intercultural skills. Although we are all affected by globalization, we associate it with different hopes, aspirations and fears. Thus, the texts assembled in this *Viewfinder* topic teach students to be aware of similarities and differences within a global society.

Texts in this book to practise your intercultural skills are:

intercultural awareness	texts 1, 4, 5, 6, 7, 16, 19, 20, 21, 22, 23, 24, 25, 26
empathizing with others	texts 9, 10, 12, 15, 16, 19, 20
socio-historical contexts	definitions and concepts of globalization: introduction, texts 1, 2, 3; English as an international language: texts 2–5; the global economy: texts 6-11; the environment: 12–13; global challenges: 13–15; migration / mobile life, tourism: 16, 18, 19, 20, 23; technology: text 17
concepts of globalization	introduction, texts 1, 6, 20, 27, 28
prejudices and stereotypes	texts 6 ('economy'),19, 22, 25
poverty and issues of equality	texts 9, 10, 11, 16

Revision

As preparation for exams and assessments, it is a good idea to revise the main points you've learnt in this *Viewfinder*. The information may be useful if you are asked questions about this topic, or as background knowledge to put things into context. And if you are sure about these points it will boost your confidence.

Key terms and concepts

Globalization
Spread of English
Global economy
Global crises
Global consumerism, globalized production
Global environment
Global challenges
Migration, immigration, global mobility
The digital revolution
Intercultural learning, intercultural awareness
Stereotypes
Critical incidents
Pros and cons of globalization

Intertextual references: famous texts, people, events

Texts

The Cambridge Encyclopedia of the English Language	text 3
The Hitchhiker´s Guide to the Galaxy (movie, book)	text 4
Painting: 'The "Little" Tower of Babel'	text 4
The Lexus and the Olive Tree	text 6
No Logo	text 9
Selling Globalization	text 11
"The Cree Prophecy"	text 12 (p. 33)
Short story: "Old Age Gold"	text 16
The Road Ahead	text 17
Paradise News	text 18
Are You Experienced?	text 19
Song: "Down Under" (Men at Work)	text 19 (23)
Pulp Fiction (film)	text 22

Contents of the Reference Library

Important differences between British and American English

Section A – Basic Skills
  A 1 Developing your receptive skills
    A 1.1 Listening comprehension
    A 1.2 Reading comprehension
  A 2 Language development techniques
    A 2.1 Processes of language acquisition
    A 2.2 Processes of language learning
        A 2.2.1 Expanding your vocabulary
        A 2.2.2 Improving your grammar (A Life-Raft of English Structure)
        A 2.2.3 Improving your pronunciation and intonation
        A 2.2.4 Improving your spelling and punctuation
  A 3 Using dictionaries
  A 4 Note-making and note-taking
  A 5 Using advance organisers (mind map, topic web, flow chart)
  A 6 Using the web
  A 7 Carrying out a project

Section B – Communication Skills
  B 1 Speaking and conversation
  B 2 Brainstorming, opinion, discussion and debate
  B 3 Survey by interview
  B 4 Presentation, paper and speech
  B 5 Role play and simulation
  B 6 Conveying the sense (in German: *Mediation*) and interpreting

Section C – Text Skills
  C 1 Analysing texts
    C 1.1 Analysing literary texts
        C 1.1.1 Poetry
        C 1.1.2 Drama
        C 1.1.3 Narrative texts (fiction)
        C 1.1.4 Points on academic writing
    C 1.2 Analysing non-literary texts
        C 1.2.1 General analysis
        C 1.2.2 Forms and elements of argument
  C 2 Analysing visual and audiovisual texts (cartoons, photographs, films)
    C 2.1 Analysing a static visual
    C 2.2 Analysing a film
  C 3 Writing texts
    C 3.1 Report
    C 3.2 Book report
    C 3.3 Letter
    C 3.4 Article
    C 3.5 Essay
    C 3.6 Summary
  C 4 Survey by questionnaire
  C 5 Translation (translation, interpreting, conveying the sense – German *Mediation*)
  C 6 Finding and using secondary sources (quotation, documentation, evaluation)

Section D – Intercultural Competence
  D 1 Developing your intercultural linguistic competence
  D 2 Developing intercultural skills and competences